TABLE OF CONTENT

MW00856854

Introduction   4

The Game Fish of Arizona   6

The Streams   11

The state of Arizona is divided north and south by the uplift of the Colorado Plateau. On the northern, uplifted side lie the state's forests, from the Christmas tree spruce-fir of the "mountain lying down," as the Navajo call the North Kaibab, to the yellow pine forests of the Mogollon Plateau and the *Sierra del Gila,* the name the Spanish gave to the unexplored mountains containing the Gila River headwaters. The famous Mogollon Rim, over 200 miles long and up to 2000 feet high, forms the northern boundary for this drainage, acting as a sort of push-off for the southern edge of the great plateau. To the south, below the rim, and beyond lesser nearby breaks in the land like the Nantac Rim and the Big Lue Mountains, lie the cactus plains and desert ranges for which the state is widely known. There the landscape is much different, resembling Mexico or, in higher elevations, the basin and range province of Nevada and Utah. Small, scattered "sky island" mountain ranges of 7000 to 9,900 feet, many covered with pine forests on their highest ridges, others merely sprinkled with junipers and oak scrub, lie in a sea of Sonoran Desert flats and mesic prairie uplands stretching all the way south to the Sea of Cortez in Mexico.

But up on the Rim, from 7000 to 8200 feet above the sea, and in the 11,000- to 12,700-foot volcanic mountains formed over it, there is no desert. Moist air masses from the Gulf of Mexico, the Sea of Cortez, and the Pacific Ocean collide with the 2000-foot uplift and spill ocean moisture over the waving expanse of ponderosa pines covering the Mogollon Plateau, the largest unbroken pine forest in the American West. Here, intense summer thunderstorms, with possibly the highest rate of lightning strikes per square mile in the world, form many springs, some filtering deep into the earth, others pouring out through cracks in the volcanic rock. Virtually all of the permanent trout waters of Arizona arise as cold springs, and most of these first emerge somewhere near the Rim. Most are high up, above 5000 feet, higher than Mt. Katahdin in Maine, or even higher, above 6500 feet, higher than Mount Mitchell in North Carolina, or higher yet, above 9000 feet, higher than all but a few mountain ranges in North America. The higher you go, the cooler it is (about 5 degrees F. for every 1000 feet of elevation gain), and also the smaller the stream; the farther down, away from the Rim, the warmer the water. Somewhere in between live the trout, having first found these spots many thousands of years ago, when there was no desert at all.

The first trout I ever caught in Arizona came from Oak Creek on a golden, late-October day, near the hamlet of Sedona. That was long ago, before much of the great exodus into what is now called the "Sun Belt." Over recent years, people from all over the world have come to Arizona, to visit and to live, by choice rather than by necessity. They have all come here, just to be in Arizona. This is understandable, but I think it was even better before. Not only was the canyon spectacular on that October day, but it felt remote, cut off from the rest of the world. Remote it no longer is, but if I were to return tomorrow, I bet I could catch another trout from exactly the same spot.

This book gives a thumbnail account of most of the roughly 330 Arizona streams which contain cold water and at least some trout, plus many of the impounded reservoirs now holding trout year round, all included in a list at the end of the book. Like all lists, this one is undoubtedly incomplete and flawed. I have fished for wild trout in more than 200 streams in the state over the past 20 years, and experience has taught that it is impossible to keep tabs on every stream every year. Many trout populations in the smaller streams are only temporary. Once depleted, usually by drought coupled with other causes, they must wait for eventual re-colonization or else timely re-stocking. Even among the larger streams, development, changes in land management, extreme natural variations in rainfall both during the year and from year to year (including a ten-year, recurring drought-to-wet cycle), and other vagaries can turn last year's great fishing into next year's disappointment, or *vice versa.* In Arizona, it seems you never find the stream exactly as you left it. Sometimes the difference is complete—the trout have either all left, or all returned. The list and text encompass all these uncertainties.

The text also describes the fish you might look for, and a small bit about insects and hatches (which are not at all crucial to success, at least not on the streams). I have tried to emphasize wild trout, thus describing mainly the streams. The stream tally is deliberately long and nearly exhaustive, to emphasize the basic point that Arizona is not one but many places, and is nearly as well suited to wild trout as it is to sun lovers. A fly fisherman can have his cake and eat it, too, finding a suitable stream and fishing for wild trout nearly year round in shirtsleeve weather. It is a land of great elevation change (12,000 feet of it), many life zones, from the subtropical to the subarctic, many hidden niches, many pleasant surprises.

Because of the Mogollon Rim, also, most of Arizona's trout streams flow roughly north to south, a lucky orientation which keeps canyons shaded and cool for much of the day. The Rim cuts northwest to southeast across the center of the state, forming a sort of centerline at the top of the drainages. Here, at the centerline, lie twenty-million acres of forest, nearly all of it publicly owned and open for your own personal

Arizona TROUT

A FLY FISHING GUIDE

Frank Amato

PORTLAND

© 1999 Rex Johnson, Jr.
ALL RIGHTS RESERVED. No part of this book may be reproduced in any means without the written
consent of the Publisher, except in the case of brief excerpts in critical reviews and articles.
Photography: Strider Brown and Jay Scott
Illustrations: Jay Scott unless otherwise noted
Maps: Ronald Smorynski
Book Design: Amy Tomlinson
Softbound ISBN: 1-57188-139-5   Softbound UPC: 0-81127-00112-5

Frank Amato Publications, Inc.
P.O. Box 82112, Portland, Oregon 97282
(503) 653-8108
Printed in Singapore

3 5 7 9 10 8 6 4 2

inspection. Since Arizona's trout streams flow north to south, and since most maps align north and south with the vertical, the streams are easier to illustrate on the pages of a book. I have arranged the major drainages in geographic order, west to east, each with an accompanying map showing streams, land features, plus major roads and trails. At the beginning and end are separate sections on the Grand Canyon and four isolated mountain ranges where trout have been transplanted and can now be caught. Each of these sections, also, has a small map. Trout streams and lakes are bold, all others subdued. Dry washes are dotted. In the text, boldface type indicates trout waters. An asterisk denotes water closed to the public (most of these are on Indian tribal lands). I have made written directions to the streams very brief. Most are at least approachable by graded Forest Service or Indian Reservation roads. All roads and trails mentioned in the text are also shown on the maps. I have tried to make the maps as uncluttered as possible. All of this helps to accomplish the first task of every trout fisherman, that of finding a stream to fish.

Cautionary Notes

Arizona is a place of extremes, where nature can be both generous and unforgiving. Backpacking and camping in the mountains can be dangerous for people inexperienced in the outdoors. Here are a few things worth remembering: In summer, dehydration is always possible. Most newcomers who hike into the lower-elevation mountains in the hot months simply do not drink enough water, and they suffer accordingly, everything from mild headaches to fatal heat stroke. Count on at least a gallon a day in the hot months. If temperatures approach or exceed 100 degrees, many people require close to two gallons.

The direct sun burns your skin. Avoid it. Use sunscreen, sunglasses, a hat. Cover yourself. If you can help it, don't exert yourself in the middle of the day, particularly between 10 a.m. and 2 p.m.

At higher elevations (7000 feet and above) there can be a 40- to 50-degree difference between daytime and nighttime temperatures. You should have a warm bag and warm clothing for the night. If you wade in a stream, use nylon shorts and heavy-duty wading sandals, which allow you to dry quickly. During the day, thunderstorms can bring freezing hail and produce an equivalent 40-degree temperature drop, as though night had fallen, within thirty minutes' time in some cases. Under these conditions, campers can suffer mild hypothermia in the high mountains in mid-summer. In spring and early summer, winds can produce the same hypothermia as low temperatures, especially if you are wet. People in the Southwest have died from hypothermia in March during rain and snowstorms in the mountains. Later in the year, in high elevations and dry air, it can be much colder or much hotter than it seems. Light-colored cotton clothing blocks the sun in the heat, while light jackets, rain gear, and long pants conserve warmth in the cold and rain.

Summer storms bring lightning bolts, which seek higher ground and strike protruding structures and objects. Avoid ridge tops and isolated trees. Bolts don't always come from directly overhead; sometimes they slant from neighboring clouds out of apparently clear skies. If lightning is nearby, assume the worst. Stay low.

Streams used by cattle abound in poison ivy. Learn to recognize and avoid it. If you are allergic, bring cortisone creme or other analgesic. Dense streamside riparian thickets (from Latin *ripa*, or riverbank) are a favorite haunt of rattlesnakes, of which Arizona has three particularly nasty species. Scorpions roam the sand and gravel of the middle elevation streambanks at evening in the warmer months. Insect repellant will help you to avoid horsefly bites that can cause your legs, neck, and feet to swell and itch maddeningly. Streamside clover hides stinging honeybees, to which a number of people are dangerously allergic. Upland desert plants have claws, as do blackberry tangles along the streams. If you like to taste water plants, learn to identify poisonous water hemlock.

The very best of Arizona's trout fishing is to be found in wilderness areas miles from the nearest road. If you plan to visit some of these remote streams, it is a good idea to buy and learn to use topographic maps of the areas you intend to fish. Until you get your sea legs, bring a companion, preferably a more experienced one, with you on your hiking trips. Try not to take a long trip with brand-new equipment. Many a good trip has been ruined by infected blisters from new boots, or by a rubbing pack or a leaking stove. Purify your water with iodine, halizone, or filtered pump. Arizona is still cattle country, and intestinal *giardiosis,* spread by their waterborne fecal matter, is truly an unforgettable experience. Some sufferers never entirely rid themselves of the infection.

Above all, fear not. Preparation, caution, and common sense will see you through every trip. Streams, after all, were meant to be explored. The hardest part of any fishing trip is getting out the door. Meanwhile, some of the state's truly superb waters rarely see a fisherman. Tight lines.

Arizona is the second most arid state, but it is a very large 114,000 square miles, it is full of mountains, and some mountain ranges receive 35 inches or more of precipitation a year. Indigenous trout populations, of a type found nowhere else in the world, have found a suitable home here for many millennia, in the headwaters of the Gila, Salt, Verde, and possibly Agua Fria Rivers, south of and almost directly under the Mogollon Rim, and in the extreme headwaters of the Little Colorado River in the White Mountains. My guess is that about two-thirds of Arizona's coldwater streams were inhabited by the native trout at the time of the first European exploration of the Southwest. There were not a great number of such streams, then or today, but what the state lacks in quantity of trout waters it more than makes up for in the great diversity of its trout habitats, their incredible fertility, and in the spectacular settings where they can be found.

Apache trout

Arizonans are fortunate in that the great majority of their cold streams lie on public lands, primarily on the state's 11-million acres of national forests, and also on certain portions of the 20 million acres of tribal lands reserved and held in trust by the federal government. Access is open to all, and were it not for this public estate, which greatly enhances Arizona's quality of life, there would be very little for a fly fisherman to write about, due to a basic scarcity of permanent water sources. Since the streams are on public lands whose management is susceptible to public pressure, every fisherman is in effect a streamkeeper, and fly fishing groups present a growing influence on the way the lands are maintained.

Such influence is needed. In many streams there is great room for improvement. I would guess that two-thirds of Arizona's trout streams are of a marginal nature, and most if not all of these streams could be improved considerably with proper restoration of their respective watersheds. The habitats have declined because they are particularly fragile—Arizona, besides being dry, is near the southerly natural limit for trout. Even so, the public lands have, on the whole, protected most streams from fatal alteration. What is more, where these public streams have been degraded restoration is at least theoretically possible through improved enforcement of the environmental laws, which protect all public lands. Two of the most widespread problems are chronic overgrazing across the state and logging practices on the Mogollon Plateau and the White Mountains. Each can destroy streams completely or lead to the loss of 50 to 90 percent of their trout populations, through indirect environmental effects such as erosion, siltation, the loss of organic food base corresponding to removal of riparian vegetation, and overall increases in water temperatures. Upland grazing, in particular, has turned a number of the state's trout streams from permanent to ephemeral, thus reducing populations by 100 percent when the streams dry up entirely. These effects stretch back over 100 years and are well known to science, yet the federal agencies have been slow to realize the value in restoring rather than cropping Arizona's natural estate.

ARIZONA'S NATIVE GAME FISH

The state fish of Arizona is the Arizona or **Apache trout**, *Oncorhynchus apache*, or according to a recent proposed re-classification, *Oncorhynchus gilae apache.* This fish has a very limited endemic range, basically the upper Salt and Little Colorado River watersheds, in waters lying just below the Mogollon Rim and upwards through the White Mountain volcanic field. These fish are found nowhere in the world but Arizona. They are a light olive-brown color on the back, shading gradually to a pale enamel or, in larger fish, a dull golden or brass color on the belly, sometimes with very faint purple iridescent bars along the sides and, always sprinkled with bright black spots. There is a dark, horizontal band through the iris of the eye, which gives the fish a masked appearance. You can usually see creamy white margins along the forward fin edges. The dorsal fin is noticeably large, the body thick and compressed. The early settlers called these trout "yellow bellies," which is as descriptive a term as any. Most of the remaining pure stocks can be found on the White Mountain Apache Indian Reservation near the New Mexico border, and the species was given its current name by Robert Rush Miller in 1972 in appreciation of efforts made by the White Mountain tribe to protect and conserve reservation stocks. In an earlier report, Miller had considered it merely to be one form of the Gila trout, still found in the mountains of neighboring New Mexico.

No one is sure exactly where this Arizona/Apache trout came from, how it evolved, or what origin it shares with its closest relatives, the three to six endemic trouts of northern Mexico and the extremely rare Gila trout still found in the mountains of neighboring New Mexico. Of the forty or so salmonids in North America (which is richest in trout species of all the continents), this particular trout of the desert mountains is neither the largest nor most spectacular, but it is of all the trouts my particular favorite. It rises to a fly as readily as any brown trout, I have caught it in sizes up to 16 inches in some incredibly tiny streams, and it has turned up repeatedly over the years, in pure or hybrid form, and often unexpectedly, in most of the waters I've fished in its original range. It grows to well over 20 inches in some White Mountain waters such as Christmas Tree Lake, where it can be a very idiosyncratic and selective feeder. It is now raised in the Alchesay and Williams Creek hatcheries in the White Mountain Apache Reservation, and reared at Silver Spring and other Arizona facilities. In the streams of the White Mountain Apache Reservation, and in the upper Black River system in the Apache National Forest, hatchery Apache trout are replacing the planted rainbows, as the Arizona Game and Fish Department gradually places a major focus on the state's native species. As a result, the Apache trout, formerly unknown to most Arizona anglers, can be caught today in increasing numbers.

The **Gila trout,** *Oncorhynchus gilae gilae,* is native to the headwaters of the Gila River proper, primarily in neighboring New Mexico, but it is also thought originally to have been found in Arizona's Verde, Agua Fria, and perhaps San Francisco River systems. The Gila and Apache trout are so similar that many taxonomists consider them to be the same species, and recent studies indicate that the Gila and Apache trout may vary less from each other than do most subspecies of cutthroat trout. The Gila trout has smaller and more profuse spots than the Apache. It also retains its lateral "redband" well into adult life, while the Apache does not. Older specimens have a yellowish to orange "cutthroat" marking similar to that of the cutthroat trout.

Arizona currently holds no accepted pure-strain Gila trout, but it may hold hybridized populations. For example, one New Mexico population of Gila trout is found in Spruce Creek, a stream emptying not into the Gila River proper but rather into the San Francisco River, a major downstream tributary of the Gila, and the Spruce Creek fish vary noticeably from the rest of the known Gila trout types. Miller, who first described the species in 1950, originally thought them to be a Gila-cutthroat hybrid, because of small "hyoid" teeth found between the gill arches in the throats of some specimens. Their coloration closely resembles that of the Apache trout, mixed with some features shown by the other *O. gilae* stocks. Meanwhile, there is a record of a variant trout form taken from KP Creek, another San Francisco River headwater near the Arizona-New Mexico line, near the turn of the century. There is also a variant still found today in Chitty Canyon, at the headwaters of Eagle Creek, which enters the Gila River just a few miles from the mouth of the San Francisco. Recent studies have shown similarities in these fish, and it is possible that the San Francisco River once held an intermediate subspecies of Gila-Apache type trout now represented by the fish in Spruce Creek.

Roundtail chub

Other Arizona tributaries of the Gila River, in particular the Verde River system, may well have held yet other sub-types, some also with "hyoid" teeth. For instance, one group of specimens taken from Oak Creek, near Flagstaff, near the turn of the century, was thought by Miller to be a hybrid of the Gila trout with the rainbow trout. It could be, instead, that these represented another variant form of the original native trout.

Taking all these factors into consideration, it might be most sensible to postulate a Gila/Apache trout species once spread into various distinct populations over all the drainages beneath the Mogollon Plateau, which feed the Gila River. These drainages all lie below and to the south of the Mogollon Rim. The similar but various trout forms found here would be the true native trout of the American Southwest.

Once the major game fish of Arizona, and essentially the state's only native game fish, the Gila and Apache trout have gradually disappeared from nearly all their original range. Both are now listed under the Endangered Species Act, but fishing for the Apache is still allowed on selected streams and small reservoirs. Both forms readily interbreed with the rainbow trout, and it is mainly

the repeated stocking of rainbows since the turn of the century into nearly every suitable source of cold water that has led to the disappearance of the natives. In the 1960s, efforts were made by the state to reverse this trend, and Apache trout were placed into a number of waters which had not held trout in historical times. Two of these, North Canyon Creek in the Grand Canyon and the Grant Creek system draining the west slope of Mount Graham, still have pure-strain populations. With passage of the Endangered Species Act in 1973, federal agencies have taken the lead in re-introduction efforts, which are now confined to waters believed to have been the original range of the two species.

The spectacularly colored **Colorado cutthroat trout,** *O. clarki pleuriticus,* was originally found in the drainages of the Chuska Mountains of extreme northeastern Arizona and adjacent New Mexico, entirely on lands within today's Navajo Indian Reservation. It has long disappeared from this extremely limited former Arizona range and is not likely to be returned to the reservation in the near future.

The **roundtail chub,** (two species, *Gila intermedia* and *Gila robusta),* a member of the cyprinid, or minnow, family, is a more recently evolved, warmwater version of the trout, and often takes its place immediately downstream from the lower limits of the trout habitats on Southwestern rivers. It has a flat, broad mouth, small, black eyes, and, despite its name, a deeply forked tail. Dull brown in color, sometimes with a very few small, faint, irregular black splotches above its lateral line, when out of the water it looks a bit like a walleye or sauger. In the water, however, it strongly resembles a trout. It sometimes seems more greenish when in the water, and when it swims rapidly it sometimes appears to have a colorful stripe along its side, not unlike that of the "rainbow" familiar to all fishermen in the West. A swift, active swimmer, the roundtail feeds enthusiastically on insects and will rise to the surface to feed on mayflies and caddisflies. For these reasons, the fish was originally dubbed the "Verde trout" by early Arizona settlers, due to its abundance in the Verde River, and also the "Gila trout" by corresponding settlers along the Gila River in southern New Mexico, which led to local confusion in the 1970s when the actual Gila trout was added to the list of endangered species. Some commentators, including W.L. Minckley from Arizona State University, have proposed that the roundtail be listed as a game fish by the state and promoted as such. Indeed, I have caught (and released) many of these fish on dry flies, often mistaking them for trout until they come to hand. The only obstacle to the roundtail's acceptance as a game fish can be found in its extremely bony flesh. Game Fish are supposed to be tasty, and the roundtail is not. Rapidly dwindling in range and numbers, it is being considered for its own listing under the Endangered Species Act.

EXOTIC SPECIES

Arizona has only one permanent natural lake, Stoneman Lake south of Flagstaff, which never contained trout or other game fish. It is fitting, then, that today the introduced, hatchery-grown **rainbow trout** is the predominant sport fish of the state's man-made ponds and reservoirs. Now re-named *Oncorhynchus mykiss,* the

North American rainbow is a native species almost entirely of Pacific coastal drainages ranging from the Alaska Peninsula to northern Baja California. It is contained in only two notable American inland river systems, the Columbia and Sacramento, and two Canadian, the Fraser and Skeena. Errant but natural populations inhabit the upper Athabasca and Smoky River drainages in Alberta, which flow eventually into the Canadian Arctic Ocean. The rainbow has a long and narrow range, essentially a band 50 to 300 miles wide along the Pacific Ocean, stretching from the sub-arctic roughly to the 30th north parallel—not really a large area. Owing to its westward movement and the eons-old piling of mountains on its leading edge, the continent's Pacific drainages are relatively short, and as one result, the rainbow has never occurred very far from the Pacific Ocean.

The *mykiss* appellation originated from a trout reported from the Kamchatka Peninsula of Siberia in the eighteenth century; subsequent analysis has shown this fish to be not greatly different from the American steelhead, which itself is a sea-going, migratory rainbow trout. The Asian rainbow has a more limited coastal range than its North American counterpart, yet both forms range far out into the ocean; the genus *Oncorhynchus* also consists notably of six other species of sea wanderers, the Pacific salmons.

The rainbow's limited natural range contrasts with the fish's propagation by man all over the globe, in both the northern and southern hemispheres, owing mainly to the ease with which it is now raised in hatcheries.

Colorado River cutthroat trout

Massive plantings of hatchery rainbows in Arizona's White Mountains in the last fifty to sixty years have given rise in some areas to a wild, nondescript population of rainbow *x* Apache trout hybrids that have all but eliminated the native trout. The hybrids are seemingly well adapted to the harsh conditions of flood and high water temperature under which the natives evolved, and they outnumber their principal competitors in these waters, the introduced brown trout. Foote Creek, Grant Creek, lower KP and Strayhorse Creeks, all in the Blue River system, plus the upper San Francisco River, the Nutrioso Creek watershed (above Springerville), and also, farther west, West Clear and Wet Beaver Creeks all contain thriving, stream-born populations of rainbows and/or hybrids. Elsewhere, hatchery-raised, 9-inch campground "catchables" are in all likelihood the most frequently caught game fish in Arizona. Some winter plantings also occur at lower elevation sites, where trout cannot live all year. Winter deposits are even made in cities like Tucson and Phoenix, even in such places as golf course water hazards (none of which, rest assured, are treated in this book).

The most famous Arizona rainbows are the giants found in the Colorado River tailwaters below Glen Canyon and Hoover Dams,

and in upper Lake Mohave. The Glen Canyon rainbows, some weighing ten to fifteen pounds, live in over 200 miles of the river and spawn in the spring creeks lying at the bottom of the Grand Canyon. They are caught with spinning tackle below Lee's Ferry. The Mohave and Hoover Dam rainbows all come from the Willow Creek federal hatchery, their lake home having no natural spawning sites in the desert washes found below the Grand Canyon. These desert trout are fished for in the manner of the steelhead and salmon that have been put into the Great Lakes, with powerboats, downriggers, and trolled spinners. This naval assault is as much a Las Vegas as an Arizona fishery.

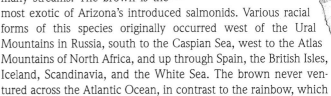

Just as the rainbow monopolizes most of Arizona's reservoirs, so, too, does the **brown trout**, *Salmo trutta*, dominate a good share of the state's moving waters, though it is no longer stocked. Wild rainbows have taken hold in most of Arizona's trout waters, but they do not dominate in many streams. The brown is the most exotic of Arizona's introduced salmonids. Various racial forms of this species originally occurred west of the Ural Mountains in Russia, south to the Caspian Sea, west to the Atlas Mountains of North Africa, and up through Spain, the British Isles, Iceland, Scandinavia, and the White Sea. The brown never ventured across the Atlantic Ocean, in contrast to the rainbow, which crossed the Pacific either directly or *via* the Bering land bridge. Somewhat analogous to the rainbow's alternate form, the steelhead, and its salmon cousin, the brown has a sea-wandering relative in the Atlantic salmon, which did cross over into North America as far inland as Lake Ontario. Although browns themselves venture into the sea, they do not generally stray far from river mouths. When transplanted, they tend not to wander downstream, as the rainbows do. In Arizona, large numbers of wild browns inhabit the middle to high elevations of most of the larger streams.

The only sections of the state where browns are rarely found are the streams draining Mount Graham, the Agua Fria River system, the uppermost San Francisco River system, the Nutrioso drainage above Springerville, west Clear Creek, the Show Low/Silver Creek drainages, and the Colorado River drainage below Lake Powell. The other watersheds contain descendants of the "Loch Leven" trout planted throughout the state from 1900 to the 1950s, all extremely successful introductions. Today, wherever rainbow trout stocking of a given stream ceases, the browns seem to solidify their hold there. Immune to heavy fishing pressure, reaching 20 inches or more in every good-condition stream of even moderate flow, they are a challenge even to the most seasoned and skillful angler.

The introduced **brook char** or brook trout, *Salvelinus fontinalis,* is found in drainages scattered throughout Arizona, but is common only in a few. Unlike the higher elevation waters in Colorado, Wyoming, and even Utah, most Arizona trout streams are not cold or high enough for brookies to take hold. Arizona's brook trout are found in the higher headwaters and impoundments of a few north-flowing streams atop the Mogollon Rim. A few headwaters under the Rim, such as upper Bonito, Ellison, and Dick Williams Creeks, also have held them from time to time. Planted brook char have taken hold in Marijalda Creek on southeastern Arizona's Mount Graham, but they recently disappeared from the neighboring Chiricahua Mountains. All told, most of the state's brookies have been stocked in reservoirs in Arizona's White Mountains, which are much higher than the rest of the state's watersheds, but even here comparatively few wild populations have become established. Those which do are found mostly near and above the 9000-foot elevation level, where they seem to

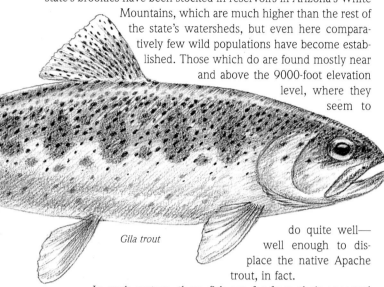

Gila trout

do quite well— well enough to displace the native Apache trout, in fact.

In such waters, these fish are far from their ancestral homes in the Appalachians, Alleghenies, the Great Lakes, Hudson's Bay region, and eastern Canada. Tolerant of lower pH levels, they generally do well in headwater streams and timberline lakes in the West, particularly in Colorado, where they predominate, but in Arizona they have not been quite so successful, possibly owing to warmer water temperatures. The state record is 4 pounds, 15 ounces from Sunrise Lake on the White Mountain Apache Reservation.

The **Arctic grayling,** *Thymallus arctus,* once found in the upper Great Lakes and the uppermost Missouri headwaters west of Yellowstone Park, but now largely confined to Alaska and northwestern Canada, has been introduced into Arizona's Bear Canyon Reservoir, Lee Valley, Lake, and Ackre Lake. The latter two populations have small spawning runs.

Other species of game fish are also available at the lower elevations — black crappie, channel and flathead catfish, largemouth and smallmouth black bass, white bass, striped bass, bluegill and green sunfish. I have caught many smallmouths and green sunfish, in particular, while looking for trout in lower-elevation stream reaches. Well-adapted, wild smallmouths are very abundant in the lower Black, slightly less so in the Verde, and are also contained in the Salt River. Most largemouths are caught in the large reservoirs near Phoenix—Saguaro, Roosevelt, and Canyon on the Salt River and Lake Pleasant on the Agua Fria are good examples—plus the middle to lower Colorado, in such waters as Lake Mead and Lake Havasu. Arizona leads the nation in per capita boat ownership, and the boats congregate along these big Colorado River and smaller Salt River reservoirs, many of them owned by bass fishermen.

SMALL STREAMS

Arizona streams are small, by anyone's definition. Some so-called "rivers" in the state can be jumped over, many "creeks" can be straddled. The major streams of the Mogollon Rim, White Mountains, and Blue Range are just large enough to allow well-placed casts from a fly rod. The tributary streams of Mogollon Mesa and the Grand Canyon are a bit smaller, with less current, and those of the Chuska, Pinaleño, and Chiricahua Mountains are nearly all as small as small can be. The Yellowstone River at Livingston, Montana is an ocean compared to such major Arizona fishing destinations as the Black River, near the New Mexico line. Of all the state's waters, only the Colorado and Salt are real rivers.

Yet what Arizona streams lack in size they more than make up for in fertility. In terms of fish biomass per streambed area, they are the best waters known, with figures two to three times as high as corresponding streams in the northern Rockies. Thus, an Arizona stream with as little as 5 cubic foot per second (cfs) of flow could be expected to hold as many fish as a Montana stream with 15 to 20 cfs. A five-acre pond here will hold as many good fish as a 10- to 15-acre lake elsewhere. Furthermore, winterkill in moving water is generally not a problem in the state, and so there is really no minimum size for an Arizona trout stream. Just add water, enough to cover a fish, and you have one. I have seen streams with as little as 1/2 cfs of flow hold trout of 10 inches or more. There is one exception to this rule, however: There is almost no minimum size for any permanent stream's qualification as trout habitat, provided that steam hasn't been ruined by removal of vegetation, grazing, excessive seasonal water diversion, or other abuses. Generally speaking, it is such degradation that causes a small stream to lose all of its water during one or more of the eight dry months of the Arizona year. Then, the stream does, indeed, become too small, and the fish disappear, not returning when the water returns. This has happened to a good number of former trout streams in the state, and will happen to many more.

Years ago, I found myself wondering whether one tiny, tiny tributary of Cave Creek in the Chiricahua Mountains named Cima Creek held any trout. Cave Creek itself had been small enough— I was shocked the first time I saw a dozen or so trout moving up a foot-wide riffle one January afternoon in the 1980s. Yet, for smallness, Cima was something else, again. I had always seen water in the stream, but since I could nearly dam it with one hand I had always ignored it. One fall day, however, I was curious enough to give it a try, as a sort of experiment. I set out to follow it upstream all the way to a waterfalls where it came off the big ridge leading north from 9950-foot Chiricahua Peak, and all the way back. It had been a dry year, and in the entire afternoon's hike of several miles I glimpsed not a single fish. Fall was passing on, and in some places up the mountain the water in Cima Creek was completely buried by piles of fallen leaves, dry on top. Most people would not think there was any stream here at all—just leaves. Anyone watching me stalking along would have thought that I was clueless, a mummer with a fly rod.

Yet on the way up, I had noted one likely pool in the lower end of the stream. As I returned from the mountain, I decided to pretend there might be a trout in it. Circling downstream, then inching slowly along the bank on hands and knees, I lay down away from the water just below the boulder and windfall which had dammed the tiny stream, completely out of sight. Ever so gently I swung my size 14 Hare's Ear Nymph forward and let it drift into the footstool-sized hole under the roots of a sycamore tree, and immediately a 13-inch brown trout flashed after it. As I stepped forward to lead the fish out of the pool and let it thrash upstream through ankle-deep water, I noticed another, slightly smaller brown darting to a hiding place under the boulder—amazing. It reminded me of turning over a log in the forest and finding two giant salamanders. Clearly, this pool was the place to go, and if I hadn't assumed something good was here and fished it blind, I would to this day believe Cima Creek to be an empty stream. What is more, there were probably other trout there in Cima Creek, other places I'd overlooked entirely. Maybe a 15-inch trout hid in one of them, or 16 or 17 inches. Believe me, it has happened; this scene has been re-played many, many times over the years in the miniature waters of the Southwest, in many streams like Cima Creek.

Mayfly nymph

The moral? Don't overlook. Even if you don't fish such a tiny, *bonsai* stream and set your sights on something a bit larger, Cima Creek serves as a good example. If there's water, don't worry, the fish are there, too. The trout have always found the place before you.

When you bring a fly rod to a stream four or five feet across or even half that width, but nonetheless filled with wary trout, the most important factor, one that outweighs all others put together, is, simply, that you must not scare the fish. I have seen large trout bolt in these waters merely from sensing footfalls on the bank, or from seeing a shadow land ten to twenty feet away. In most streams you must not allow yourself to see the fish, even with your fancy sunglasses. Sooner or later the fish will turn and see you, too. It takes very little time to learn to guess where in the stream the fish are going to be—they live in hiding places where the deepest possible pools of water form. Depth and structure are what they always seek, both together.

Having trained yourself not to spook the fish with your presence, your second rule is not to spook the fish with your cast. Many times I have seen a startlingly big trout right in the middle of the stream feeding on everything that comes its way, with no way to catch it. The only way not to disturb a big trout feeding in micro-water is not only to allow a small nymph or dry pattern to drift by, but also to cast it so that it doesn't land within view or at least doesn't make a ripple when it lands. Sometimes there is not enough room or current to do this, and in such cases I just leave the fish alone, hoping that when I return it will have moved to a more fishable spot. If a landing fly disturbs the water in any way, the trout is gone, however, and won't soon be seen again. Dry flies scare the fish far less than the splash of a nymph as it falls into a still pool. When I fish with dry flies in Arizona, it is generally on a tiny stream where anything else will disturb the water. Normally I choose nymphs first, this because the fish are seldom truly selective, and probably also because I have become so used to fishing blind. I would rather feel a strike than watch it—easier on the eyes, in the blinding sun.

Stonefly nymph

The best time to fish the smallest streams is July and August, for a simple reason. During the summer "monsoon" season you are able to wait for the stream to cloud a bit after heavy rains. This hides the fish from you, and you from the fish. Arizona gets the greater share of its yearly precipitation in July and August, when thunderstorms create downpours, or at least brief showers, nearly every afternoon. These rains swell and roil the streams, but generally help rather than hinder the fishing. Often a stream is too small to fish before the rains. In June, many streams are so low that their current actually disappears. Whatever flow of water remains in the stream passes beneath the ground, and the fish seem to be living in tiny, discrete, stagnant pools scooped out of the gravel. The water is not stagnant, however. It is cold and fresh, being now a certain type of insulated groundwater. The stream becomes a kind of spring. The trout survive this low water, but the stream is almost unfishable. Then, when the rains come in July, current resumes, the water colors slightly, insect activity reaches a maximum, and the trout become bold. The stream is now fishable again, and results are often excellent.

INSECTS, HATCHES, AND LURES

Though lake fish can be very choosy in late summer and stream fish tend to follow the *Baetis* in winter months, there are few times in Arizona streams when you absolutely have to match a hatch to catch a trout. In the larger streams there are usually a variety of insect forms available in the water column, and so selective feeding seldom occurs. Few forms are ignored completely, but some others are often preferred. A brief list of these would include dobsonfly larvae for lower-elevation streams, especially those which also hold bass, grasshoppers and other terrestrials for dry fall weather through November, blue damselflies for the lakes through June. In higher-elevation streams, the mayflies are dominated by the squat, clinging *heptageniidae* family, seconded by the *Baetis* swimmers. For *Baetis* the blue-winged olive is universal, number 16. For the others you use a small blue quill for the dark forms, and the pale evening duns for most of the rest. For the caddisflies all summer, "fish the Adams, ignore the hatch." *Isoperla* (yellow) and *Amphinemura* (brown) stoneflies, both small, are occasional in higher waters in June and July, for which you can use the corresponding nymph patterns, preferably number 8 or 10.

Finally, the wingless life stages of all water insects are those most often fed upon by Arizona's stream trout. Disregarding all other forms, you could catch perhaps five hundred trout or more during any given summer using only a number 14 natural hare's ear nymph, with a bead-head when needed for deeper pools or faster water. To quote John Keats, "This is all ye know, and all ye need to know."

1. THE GRAND CANYON

Name: Colorado River
Location: Glen Canyon National Recreation Area, Grand Canyon National Park, Hualapai and Havasu Indian Reservations, Lake Mead National Recreation Area, Mohave and Coconino Counties
Maps: Kaibab National Forest Visitors Map, North Kaibab Districts; USGS 1:100,000 series, Tuba City, Grand Canyon, Glen Canyon Dam, and Mount Trumbull
Elevation: 3000-1900 feet
Length of Trout Water: 264 miles
Best Times: November-April
Fish Species: Rainbow trout, brook char (very rare)
Tributaries: North Canyon Creek, Nankoweap Creek, Unkar Creek, Vishnu Creek, Clear Creek, Bright Angel Creek, Roaring Springs, Phantom Creek, Crystal Creek, Pipe Creek, Monument Creek, Hermit Creek, Crystal Creek, Dragon Creek, Shinumo Creek, White Creek, Royal Arch Creek, Tapeats Creek, Thunder River, Deer Creek, Havasu Canyon, Diamond Creek

I have never read an adequate description of the Grand Canyon, and I won't attempt to give one here, except to say that it is exceptionally big (from the Latin *grandis*, "big"), and it was carved by the **Colorado River** (*colorado* being Spanish for "colored," usually red). Formerly, the brick-colored river used naturally eroded desert sediments as a cutting tool, and contained desert river fish amazingly well-adapted to the heavy, silty currents and seasonal floods. The damming of Glen Canyon in 1963 fundamentally changed the nature of the lower river and its fish habitats—a wildly fluctuating desert warmwater stream was transformed into a tightly controlled, 54-degree tailwater. Five native minnow species almost immediately disappeared, including the Colorado squawfish, a predatory minnow sometimes weighing over 100 pounds and called "salmon" by early Arizona settlers. In place of the natives, rainbow trout were planted at the old Mormon crossing at Lee's Ferry, below the dam, much as they had been planted from the federal hatchery at Willow Beach into the Lake Mead tailwaters and upper Lake Mohave in the 1940s, after completion of Hoover Dam. The state record rainbow, 21 pounds 5 ounces, was taken a few miles below that dam in 1966.

The results below Glen Canyon in the late 1960s and early 1970s were just as explosive as they had been earlier at Willow Beach, providing for a legendary rainbow trout fishery, the amazing growth of the younger fish based largely on amphipods, or "freshwater shrimp." Seven-fish limits of over 100 pounds of salmon-red trout flesh were not unheard of in the 1970s. Fishing for trainbows continues today, mostly by spincasters, though the trout recently have become somewhat fewer and smaller—three-to four-pounders, rather than ten-pounders, are now the aim. The tailwaters immediately below the dam are the most accessible and get the great majority of the pressure. Rafters and hikers take rainbows all the way down the Grand Canyon, past the Havasu and Hualapai Indian Reservations (tribal permits required), until Lake Mead and the Mohave Desert sun make the waters too warm.

SPRING CREEKS IN THE GRAND CANYON

Going for trout in some of the twenty or so amazing spring creeks at the bottom of the Grand Canyon qualifies as "extreme fishing," requiring either a long raft trip into the canyon (it's almost impossible to do this without signing up on one of the tours, with rigid schedules), or a sort of reverse Everest climbing expedition down into the canyon itself, occasionally without means of a trail. This in itself wouldn't be so bad, perhaps, if it weren't for the insane heat at the canyon bottom on the one hand, which you have to accommodate nine or ten months of the year, and the snow, relative inaccessibility, and unpredictable weather of much of the North Rim in the winter, on the other. As a result, the limestone spring streams of the Grand Canyon are a delight relatively few people have ever experienced, or perhaps ever will.

NORTH RIM

Unlike the Willow Beach rainbows, which have nowhere to spawn, those introduced below Glen Canyon Dam after the reservoir filled in the late '60s quickly found suitable redd sites in a number of the spring creeks, and promptly took over these streams, also. The most notable, **Bright Angel Creek**, 14 miles of ice cold and crystal-clear trout habitat, had held wild browns for decades, but the big spawning rainbows unleashed below the damsite provided a bit too much stress. Today, Bright Angel, very brief **Roaring Springs**, and lower, 4-mile tributary **Phantom Creek** are a rainbow fishery *par excellence*; these are all worked by anglers—quite heavily, too, considering you have to climb at least part of the way down into the 4000-foot canyon just to start fishing. From the campground at Bright Angel point on the North Rim to where the creek meets the river is a descent of about 3200 feet, the descent to Cottonwood Camp part-way down the canyon is only 2000. This climb out is a lot more enjoyable in February than in June or even April. In the summer, temperatures along the creek are well over 100 degrees, but the water stays ice-cold and beautifully clear all year long—this is an enormous, subterranean limestone spring, full of trout where it emerges.

At much smaller, 4-mile **Clear Creek**, ten miles to the east of Bright Angel and reachable over a rough trail from Bright Angel's lower end, the water is so comparatively small, and the rainbows so comparatively big during the spring spawning run, that fishing at this time is extremely difficult—no room. This stream is seldom visited by fishermen because Bright Angel is usually good enough to discourage further exertions.

Generally unfishable in summer, when its open valley and black-rock bottom warms the water to bathtub temperatures, the stream's trout return each winter to feed. Next come **Vishnu and Unkar creeks**, each about 2 miles long, accessible from the river. Vishnu is 6 miles upriver from Clear Creek, Unkar about 15. Each is equivalent to Clear in fishing character, but trail-less, more remote, and fishable later in summer. Access is from the river. Much, much farther upstream, in the Marble Canyon section of Grand Canyon National Park, **Nankoweap Creek** enters. This is a bit bigger stream, 6 or so miles long, but hard to ascend; only the last 200 yards or so above the Colorado are easily negotiable, because of steep chutes and rapids. For best results, fish all these streams from November to April.

North Canyon Creek is a tiny "upland" Grand Canyon stream, in that it forms on the Kaibab Plateau from rainfall and small upland seeps, not deep springs, and it turns into a dry wash long before reaching the Colorado. Formerly barren, its upper reach was planted with Apache trout in the 1970s because of its isolation from the river. Like most streams down in the canyon, it crosses no road, but it has a trail and is easily reachable by a good hike. The descent is more than 3000 feet for the five miles from FR 610 and 611, near Deer Lake on the North Rim road (AZ 67), to the lower limit of the trout water. Due to the topography, however, there is ample shade here, in the forest zone of the Kaibab. Few people try this stream; it is the only real trout water in the Kaibab National Forest, deeply shaded by alders and willow thickets, and flowing within the Saddle Mountain Wilderness Area.

About 9 miles downstream from Bright Angel Creek lies 5-mile **Crystal Creek**, entering the river just above Crystal Rapids, and its 1-mile tributary **Dragon Creek**. No trails here; you enter the creek from the river only, say during a rafting expedition, wading and climbing upstream for three to five miles, if you are so inclined. Few people ever do this, especially since most can pick up a few 15-inch rainbows right where they beach their raft. Most tourists, even avid fishermen, find themselves asking the question, "Why fish in the creek for the grandchildren of the trout I can catch right here?" In the case of 4-mile **Shinumo Creek** and its tributary, 5-mile **White Creek**, entering the river roughly 10 miles below Crystal mouth, climbing up the stream would be even harder. Upstream passage on this stream system is no easy proposition. Very few fishermen (including me) have ever been here.

If you want to try to hike into possibly the most unlikely stream in Arizona, so remote that you'll be "hell and gone," as the old-timers say, try **Thunder River**, but don't try it in the summer. This very short 1/2-mile stream empties into 4.5-mile-long **Tapeats Creek** and gets its name from its enormous, roaring source spring, the biggest cold spring in the Southwest. Thunder Springs gushes out of the north wall of the Grand Canyon, forming several waterfalls. If you see this spring you'll never forget it. Tapeats has its own big spring, not nearly as noisy. No licquer or elixir on earth can compare to cold spring water on a 100-degree day. To get to Thunder, you can start at the monument Park Trailhead at the end of rough Kaibab Forest route 292A (off FR 425 near Big Saddle Point). From here you follow the "Bill Hall Trail" straight down. In about a mile you meet the Thunder River Trail. The going is so crooked it's hard to measure, but probably about 9 miles in all, starting at 6400 feet and descending to about 3300 feet at Thunder Spring; from here you need to climb down, to about 2500 feet, to get where Thunder joins Tapeats, among

oak scrub and willow thickets. Almost the entirety of the south-facing trail is exposed to the sun—unbelievably hot in the warm months. There are two makeshift camping spots on Tapeats below the Thunder's roar.

Just 3 miles below Tapeats Creek, 2.9-mile **Deer Creek**, the least used of all the north canyon streams, enters the Colorado via another impressive falls, the biggest in the park. Sadly, there are no rainbows in the stream above. There is a well-marked fork in the Thunder River Trail, just before the climb down to Thunder Springs. The fork leads to Deer Creek via tributary Deer Spring, just about a mile above the big falls.

Kanab Creek, over 100 miles long, is a muddy, flood-prone desert wash originating on the Paunsaugant Plateau in southern Utah (where it also holds wild trout). Its extreme lower end within the national park holds water year round and provides habitat for carp, suckers, plus an occasional rainbow trout from the river. The best fishing is right at the mouth. Lush Shower Bath Springs, originally named by John Wesley Powell, lies about 8 twisting miles above the Colorado and approximates the upstream limit of Kanab's permanent water. Getting into Kanab Canyon isn't easy. The least confusing way is to start at Jumpup Point in the Kaibab National Forest, at the dead end of very rough FR 204, or to the Sowats Point Trailhead at the end of FR 233. You'll find rough, hard-to-follow trails down both Jumpup and Sowats canyons. It's about 4 days round-trip to the Colorado and back, if you're in good shape. It's a great slot canyon to explore, but don't make the trip merely for the sake of a few stray trout in the lowermost mile or two.

SOUTH RIM STREAMS

Royal Arch (.5 miles), **Pipe** (1.5 miles), **Monument** (1.4 miles), **Garden** (2 miles), and **Hermit** (1.7 miles) **creeks** all enter the canyon from the South Rim, forming on the lower and drier Coconino Plateau. These are all much smaller streams than their counterparts on the other side, but they have wild rainbow trout, and they are also a bit shadier to boot. All except Royal Arch are accessible by trail from and lie directly below the busy tourist complex stretching from Mather Point to Hermits Rest. Royal Arch is remote, accessible by the river, or possibly by a climb down from the Apache Point trail, which follows the South Rim. Inquire at the Pasture Wash Ranger Station about reaching the rim and trail.

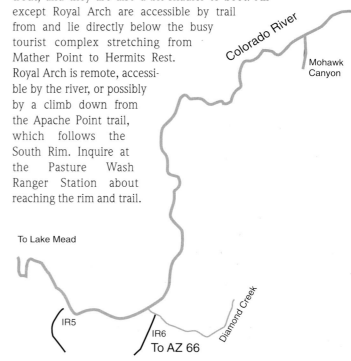

Havasu Creek in Cataract Canyon has an Indian settlement in its path, plus 11 miles of enormous, ice-cold flow, beautiful, milky, blue-green water impregnated with limestone-derived calcium carbonate, capable of growing rainbow trout rapidly to great sizes. This is not unusual for the springs of the region. The soda here is more concentrated, however, turning the canyon bottom into a sort of hardpan material and producing a sequence of travertine terraces. One result of this is an almost complete lack of suitable spawning sites. The stream must live by regular plantings of rainbow trout, which have declined recently. As a result, far fewer trout fishermen visit Havasu Canyon today than in the past, and there are fewer fish to be found. The rainbows seem to be retreating downstream, to the river, dropping below the various waterfalls, some of which, like Havasu and Mooney falls, have been photographed and shown the world over. This is the reverse of what many of the other streams experienced after Glen Canyon Dam closed,

Creek's extreme head on the Coconino Plateau, lies **Russell Tank**, 1 acre, 7000 feet. This stock pond is in the middle of nowhere in the Coconino Plateau, on Coconino National Forest Road 310 southeast of the Grandview Lookout, then on FR 311 for two miles. Rainbow trout have been planted here from time to time by Arizona Game and Fish.

many becoming natural nurseries for the river fish. Of course, there are still plenty of rainbows at the stream's mouth.

Farther downstream on Hualapai tribal lands, **Diamond Creek** has cool water in its lower reaches and about 8 miles of permanent flow. Trout can be found near the mouth and occasionally in the lower end. A number of other small springs flow near the mouths of canyons in the Hualapai lands, sometimes with stray trout. This is also the case for springs even farther downstream, below the Shivwits Plateau. There is a well-maintained tribal road from Peach Springs, Arizona, to the river, just below the mouth of Diamond Creek.

Not all the Grand Canyon trout lie in fast water at the bottom of the canyon. Up on the very divide of the South Rim at Havasu

2. AGUA FRIA RIVER SYSTEM

Name: Agua Fria River
Location: Prescott National Forest
Elevation: 3500-1400 feet
Average Flow: 35 cfs at Sycamore Creek confluence; varies seasonally, from 389 cfs in March to as little as 0.1 cfs in September; the highest recorded was 33,000 cfs in February, 1980
Length: 50 miles total, with many dry reaches
Fish Species: Green sunfish, longfin dace, fathead minnows, mosquitofish, Sonoran suckers
Fishable Tributaries: Year-round fishing in Sycamore Creek

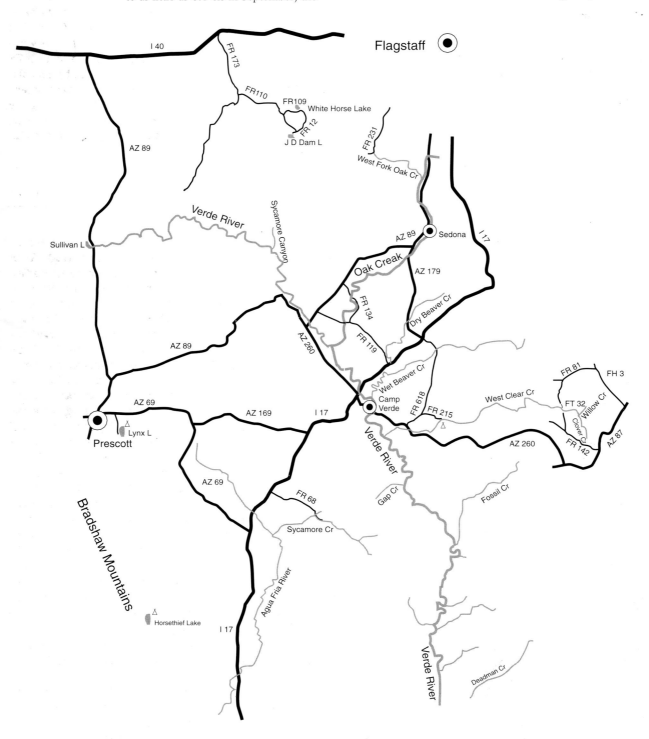

AGUA FRIA AND VERDE RIVER SYSTEM

The **Agua Fria River** is a mid-elevation desert stream draining the piñon-studded Sierra Prieta, Bradshaw and Mingus mountains, just out of Prescott, and the Black Hills to the east. The town of Prescott itself lies almost at the head of the river, at 5355 feet. Agua Fria is often dry and holds very few if any trout, but the 55-acre **Lynx Lake** impoundment, at the head of the generally dry, former-gold-rush tributary Lynx Creek, holds rainbows at 5530 feet, while **Horsethief Lake**, of similar size, holds rainbows at the headwaters of another dry tributary, Black Canyon, at 6100 feet. The lower end of the river is impounded to form Carl Pleasant Reservoir, home of a population of good-sized white bass. These are kept from becoming overcrowded and stunted by the fact that in the frequent dry years there isn't enough water in the lower river to allow a spawning run. A *Field & Stream* national prize-winning largemouth bass was caught here years ago.

The major coldwater habitat in the Agua Fria watershed is a 7-mile stretch of **Sycamore Creek**, a stream rising on the slopes of 6800-foot Pine Mountain, named after stringers of virgin pon-derosa pine extending down into the canyon of the south fork of the creek. This is a low-lying, desert mountain with pine trees on top and a spring-fed trout stream below—hard to believe, but true. Precipitation here is 20 to 25 inches of rain a year— quite a bit for Arizona, but the relatively low elevation of the creek (4000-5000 feet) makes for high heat and quick evaporation. Sycamore has about a median flow of about 2 cfs. First stocked with rainbows in the early 1940s, it is thought to have originally contained Gila or Gila-type trout at the turn of the century—also hard to believe, but also probably true. What is more, this native trout has actually survived, after a fashion. Specimens taken from the stream in 1975 have been identified as possible Gila-rainbow hybrids by trout-olo-gists Robert Behnke and M. Zarn. Arizona has dozens and dozens of creeks and canyons named Sycamore, but only two hold game fish. This particular Sycamore Creek has always been tiny, overlooked and lightly fished; yet it can be quite good in the fall, in high-rainfall years.

3. WEST VERDE SYSTEM

Name:	Verde River
Location:	Prescott National Forest, Apache and Graham Counties, Arizona
Maps:	Prescott, Coconino National Forest visitors maps
Elevation:	6000-3900 feet
Average Flow:	200 cfs at Clarkdale
Length:	125 miles
Best Times:	April, May, September-November
Fish Species:	Channel catfish, largemouth bass, smallmouth bass, bluegill sunfish, common carp, roundtail chub, spikedace, razorback sucker, rainbow trout (rare)
Tributaries:	Sycamore Canyon (trout rare), Oak Creek, West Fork Oak Creek, Wet Beaver Creek, Dry Beaver Creek (trout rare), West Clear Creek, Clover Creek, Gap Creek (trout extremely rare), Fossil Creek (bass only)

The **Verde River** is a very big stream, at least by Arizona standards, arising suddenly in the Chino Valley north of Prescott, where it receives underground flow from the porous volcanic drainfields of the weather-making,12,700-foot San Francisco Peaks. People in Flagstaff often look up at the snowfields on "the Peak," as it is called locally, and complain, "All that snow, and no water." Well, there is water, pure and filtered, passing far beneath the mountain, and it's called the Verde River. All the Verde's major tributaries and nearly all of its flow arise from the east, from "the Peak" and other smaller mountains nearby, and from the Rim, which stretches to the southeast.

Near the Prescott National Forest boundary east of the village of Paulden, the Verde is a small stream wending its way through an open valley, soon meeting the mouth of Arizona's mini-Grand Canyon at **Sycamore Creek** (which holds bass). The middle portion, from Clarkdale to the mouth of Red Creek (dry, no fish), accepts the cooler waters of **Oak Creek**, a spectacular redrock backdrop for many a 1950s cowboy movie, then passes warmwa-ter **Fossil Creek** (bass, sunfish) and coldwater **East Verde River** just before meeting the foot of the big, nasty and nearly roadless 8000-ft. Mazatzal Range and emptying into Horseshoe Reservoir north of Phoenix. Part of the middle section, from just below Clarkdale to the mouth of Red Creek, has been designated a national "Wild and Scenic River" — the only such designation in Arizona to date. The most frequently sought game fish in the river is the channel catfish, but sunfish and both smallmouth and largemouth bass are also available. Almost gone are the roundtail and Gila chubs, *Gila robusta*. These were once called the "Verde trout," because of their trout-like habits. Real Verde trout, of the exotic rainbow variety, are very hard to find, hanging at the mouths of cool-water tributaries or streamside springs. Today, if you raft or canoe the river, you are asked to kill all your bass and catfish, in order to assist the recovery of the native warmwater species.

Most likely you will not catch trout, however. The scarcity of trout lies not with water purity—the Verde is exceptionally clean for such a large, low-elevation stream— but with water temperatures, which often climb above the 80-degree mark. Trout reproduction is practically nil here, and very few of the planted rainbows survive in the Verde for even one calendar year. In high-water periods some rainbows get flushed down from the tributaries, which do hold trout, and other rainbows are stocked when the water is cool. Most streams of this elevation along the rim do not hold trout unless their canyons are very narrow, preferably flowing in a north-south direction, both of these factors help keep the water better shaded during the day. The upper Verde River has neither advantage.

The upper Verde sees regular floods which sweep back its riparian vegetation; in between floods the stream appears to re-colonize at the mouths of well-vegetated side canyons like Wet Bottom and Sycamore Creeks, which provide remnants of the once common but now quite scarce Goodding willow- Fremont cottonwood river *bosque*. (Spanish for "forest"). Elsewhere, the riverbed remains gravelly with many nearly bare points and bars;

occasional reeds, salt cedar, and mesquite clumps appear along the middle and lower river banks. Sycamores, hackberry, and ash trees also appear on low-lying benches. It gets hot here, and the catfish grow big. Trout are stocked in the winter in a 7- to 10-mile reach of the stream, in the vicinity of Camp Verde, providing a boon for fly fishers from the Phoenix area, many of them retired from Michigan and Pennsylvania seeking Arizona's warmth. *"Olden folke ben alway colde"*—Chaucer

Spectacular **Sycamore Canyon**, its stream mentioned in bold-face previously, uncovers most of the same ancient rock strata as the well-known Grand Canyon of the Colorado some 80 miles to the north, minus the millions of visitors. Up on top, at the head of its long, narrow drainage, two small impoundments, 30-acre **Whitehorse Lake** at 7000-feet and 6-acre, 6460-feet **JD Dam**, can be reached over passable dirt roads (FR 110 and 109). Whitehorse provides stocked rainbows and an occasional brown trout. JD has browns and a no-bait rule. The canyon, 24 miles long and almost 3000 feet deep, most of it contained in the Sycamore Canyon Wilderness, is very similar to the neighboring

Oak Creek Canyon, except it is bone dry for almost its entire length. Finally, the blazing hot canyon forms a pure stream when powerful, stream-sized **Parsons Springs** comes to life four miles above the Verde River confluence. The temperature of the big springs hovers above 70 degrees, which makes for a warmwater fishery containing roundtail chubs, longfin and speckled dace, the federally threatened spikedace, plus smallmouth bass and green sunfish. Trout are *muy poco* ("very few"), mostly Verde winter plant refugees. Both the springs and most of the fishing lie within the wilderness, above the private mining company land at the stream's mouth. Special regulations here forbid camping along the water, especially the springs. Locals fish this water regularly, outlanders hardly ever.

Oak Creek

Just below Sycamore Canyon, **Oak Creek** enters the Verde. This is a big, spring-fed trout stream, 50 miles long, averaging 82 cfs in its upper end, and probably the most heavily-fished in the state of Arizona. It is certainly the most photographed, flowing crystal clear over shocking, rust-red bedrock beneath distant eroded red towers and lush streamside forests, and paralleled by a busy paved tourist drive above the high-end retirement-cum-*artiste* community of Sedona. Like Sycamore, the rugged, 1000-foot Oak Creek Canyon gets its water from deep springs filtering down from the San Francisco Peak snowfields, but here the Sterling Springs give flow to Oak Creek far upstream from the Verde, as opposed to the four miles of flow for Sycamore below Parsons Springs. The state of Arizona has built a hatchery at Sterling Springs, where Apache trout had been raised since 1963, but all these were destroyed by vandals in the late 1970s. Oak Creek has brook, brown, and rainbow trout, the browns and brookies persisting mainly by natural reproduction, the wild rainbows supplanted by stockings from the downstream Page Springs facility for most of the year. Fishing is year-round; the lower 20 miles are primarily a mixed fishery with good populations of smallmouth bass. Bass are also present in the upper reaches, but in fewer numbers.

Originally, Oak Creek was home to a Gila-type trout. Specimens were collected and preserved in the 1890s, and a remnant population persisted well into the 1930s. One angler in 1930 was so impressed with an Oak Creek native trout he landed that he carved its outline onto a streamside log. What did the fish look like? Here's an excerpt from a 1959 edition of *Arizona Highways* Magazine: *At the turn of the century this highly-colored trout, which was native to our mountain streams, was our only game fish, and something to brag about, too, with his brilliant yellow belly and sideshading up to just a hint of rainbow pastels to a dark, olive-green back, and spotted with irregular dots of black.*

In the 1950s, it was not uncommon to find five or six anglers sharing the same roadside hole, especially after the stocking truck had made its rounds. Today's fishermen gravitate more towards the lakes in the area, south of Flagstaff, and "water play," as the Forest Service calls it, has taken over many pools. Below Sedona, where the water is less crowded, you can be alone on the stream, wading for bass and occasional stray browns or rainbows.

Damselfly nymph

Oak Creek has a major tributary, the **West Fork**, which flows through the Red Rock-Secret Mountain Wilderness, in a narrow and in some places claustrophobic redrock canyon of its own. Willows line the streamside, boxelders and ferns crowd the narrow benches, moss clings to clefts in the red, cinnamon, and amber-colored rock. The uppermost canyon is still wild, and the rest still beautiful. Wild browns hold here in 11 miles of water, with a very few remaining stream-born brookies in the upper end. There are also roundtail chubs, speckled dace, plus desert and Sonoran suckers. A number of rainbow trout venture into the lower canyon, as well.

More people hike the West Fork with each passing year—up to 5000 per month at the last count, and occasionally 1000 visitors on a single day, of the sub-species *Homo sapiens alienus*, sporting the latest in showy yuppie outdoor gear. Fortunately, most of these turn back after a mile or less of exploration. Horses are forbidden, and camping and campfires are now prohibited on the lower 6 miles of the canyon. This helps, but the canyon is so narrow that it seems crowded with even a few people within view. It is one of many former wilderness streams in the state I no longer fish, preferring more to live in the past, yet most anglers are not nearly as allergic to fellow anglers and hikers as I happen to be.

Most serious anglers who fish the West Fork end to end drive to the head and hike down. The upper reaches of the canyon have no trail—it is too narrow for one—and so you must pick your way and wade frequently, scaring many fish in the process. In the middle third of the canyon you have to swim across more than one deep hole. Hiking the other way, from AZ 89A (an Arizona "Scenic Highway") upstream to the Forest Service two-track (FS 231) above Buzzard Point, works better, but the climb out is a heart-buster. All in all, it's hard to share the West Fork. Try it in late September or October when you really have to want to wade it.

WET BEAVER CREEK

Next, entering the Verde twelve miles below Oak Creek, is the mouth of **Wet Beaver Creek.** This stream has a 35-mile-long course, starting from the Mogollon Rim and draining westward to the Verde River. Most of the lower stream below the state road (AZ 179) crossing is on private land and sprawling summer home developments, typical of the New West, although the two miles immediately below Montezuma Castle National Monument is public and holds warmwater species. Upstream from AZ 179, Wet Beaver Creek provides a mixed fishery on 14 miles of public lands. This is all spring-fed, crystal-clear permanent flow. The flow is considerable, averaging 35 cfs in the middle reach below Casner Butte, but dropping a bit below that in dry years. All told, Wet Beaver is one of the dozen or so largest trout streams in the state.

Nearly all of the public reach of the stream lies within the Wet Beaver Wilderness. Surrounded and disguised by drab hillsides of juniper scrub, the uppermost canyon is particularly wild, extremely steep and narrow, the red sandstone streambed fed by a sequence of cold springs. Ash, walnut, grape arbors, and willow thickets provide a canopy for the water. In amazing contrast to the residential developments below, upper Wet Beaver is seldom visited and seldom fished. The canyon is narrow, with more than 20 deep holes that require swimming to get through. Here can be found an excellent population of roundtail chubs, speckled dace, desert and Sonoran suckers, longfin dace—all native species—plus exotic largemouth and smallmouth bass, yellow and black bullhead, and red shiner, not to mention brown and rainbow trout of up to 20 inches.

Access through the permanent waters is by foot. The lowermost end is reachable by AZ 179 and forest service roads 121 and 618, which latter leads to a small campground on the creek.

Dry Beaver Creek, not entirely dry, is the only notable tributary of Wet Beaver Creek, heading in the Munds Mountain Wilderness southeast of Sedona, and joining Wet Beaver just above the Verde River confluence. In the dry months its water contracts to a few isolated pools, some of which hold minnows, smallmouth bass, and, rarely, a few trout in the upper reaches. The stream is not stocked, and fish ascend it from Wet Beaver below.

WEST CLEAR CREEK

Entering the Verde from the east about eight miles below Wet Beaver Creek, **West Clear Creek** is a sort of larger sibling to the other creek, providing 40 miles and an average of 67 cfs of permanent coldwater flow. This is major trout habitat, one of the finest wild trout streams in the Southwest.

Once called the "Clear Fork" of the Verde, as recently as 1934 the stream still held what one observer called "blue-spotted" native trout. Amazingly, although collections were made near the turn of the century, not one specimen of this original population was ever preserved or adequately photographed. These native fish were Gila-type trout, *Oncorhynchus gila spp.*, probably identical to the native trout observed and obtained from neighboring Oak Creek at the turn of the century, also long gone. In the 1940s a "trout tramway" was built to stock the stream from the north rim at the head of the canyon, complete with guest register filled with fish stories and a half-mile trail descending 1000 feet to the stream. Today the trail, FT 32, is still there, reachable by FR 81, primitive 81E, and two-rutted 142F, leading southwest from the state highway (AZ 209) about eight miles south of Happy Jack. Based on these early plantings, West Clear today provides a notable wild rainbow fishery.

The whole stream, especially in its lower portions, lies in a sort of double gorge, giving deep shade. A break in the Mogollon Plateau forms a first broad canyon, which gives way to a narrow ribbon of water and broadleaf forest sunk beneath the rimrock at the very bottom.

To fish this stream, you'll have to hike, wade, and, in some 30 or so narrow canyon spots, swim. Some pools are 20 feet deep. Access to the fishing water is by foot, either upstream from the Clear Creek Forest Service Campground five miles east of Camp Verde, at Bull Pen Ranch via spur road FR 25 which meets the canyon 6 miles above the campground, or downstream from AZ 87 at the head of the stream. A few other trails lead down into the canyon from rough forest roads above. These are shown on the Coconino National Forest Visitors Map, and you should check locally before trying them. Once in the canyon you're on your own. Watch your ankles.

There is no road crossing, just a sequence of primitive trails, from the campground area all the way upstream past the juncture of **Clover** and **Willow creeks**, to Clover Springs, where West Clear system actually begins. The upper canyon passes beneath ridges clad in ponderosa pine and occasional stands of Douglas fir, which spill down into the canyon along its cool south wall. The streamside is choked with beargrass, sawgrass, willows, wild grapevines (some as big as tree saplings), plus occasional walnut trees at close to their maximum size—nearly fifty feet tall in some places. Douglas fir trees lean out from small clefts in cliff faces, shading the water.

In great contrast to this scene are the lower reaches of the canyon, which pass out of the forest zone entirely. The stream itself is more desert-like; mesquite, catclaw, scrub oak, and prickly pear cactus line the surrounding hillsides, and the streamside plant community here includes Arizona sycamore and giant alders, mixed with the triangular-leaved Fremont cottonwoods that mark water everywhere in the Arizona desert. Wildlife abounds, including blackhawks, bear, lion, beaver, waterfowl, deer, elk, goshawks, kingfisher and heron, wintering bald eagles.

Whether you fish the upper or lower reaches of the canyon, you can catch and release fifty or more stream-born rainbow trout in an afternoon's fishing, including, if you're lucky, a couple in the 14-inch range.

Tiny **Gap Creek**, along with Red Creek one of the few measurable streams flowing into the Verde from the west, heads in the low-elevation Black Hills which crowd the west bank of the river. Gap Creek received a planting of the endangered Gila trout in 1972, but floods in the early 1980s washed many over the stream barrier built to protect them. Following the dry years of 1989 and 1990, the fish disappeared. Possibly, the stream dried up completely.

Fossil Creek enters the Verde in the Mazatzal Wilderness just above the mouth of the East Verde River. A big, coldwater stream at its source in the Fossil Springs Wilderness, Fossil Creek has the same high carbonate content as Havasu Canyon, with the same lack of spawning sites. As a result, though the enormous, aqua green Fossil Springs provides 45 cfs of pure water in the 60-degree range, there are no trout. Bass from the Verde River do show up in the downstream sections of the creek. Nearly all the stream water is diverted just below the springs (see the section on the East Verde River, page 19).

Deadman Canyon, flowing out of the Mazatzal Mountains, roadless, trail-less, and too remote for regular visits, much less fish stockings, has cold flow, but mainly speckled dace and roundtail chubs. It has never been stocked and has only recently been inventoried by AZG&F.

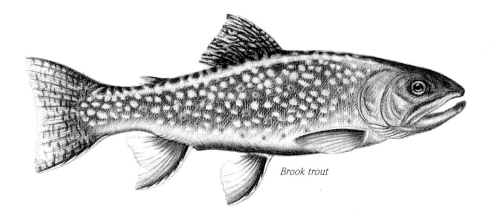

Brook trout

4. East Verde Drainage

Name:	East Verde River
Location:	Mazatzal Wilderness, Tonto National Forest,
Elevation:	7000-3900 feet
Average Flow:	Approximately 29 cfs
Length:	42 miles
Best Times:	April, May, September-November
Fish Species:	Brook char, brown trout, rainbow trout, Sonoran sucker, longfin dace, roundtail chub, razorback sucker, desert sucker, green sunfish, smallmouth bass
Fishable Tributaries:	Pine Creek, Webber Creek, Bray Creek, Sycamore Creek, Ellison Creek, Chase Creek, Dude Creek, Bonita Creek, Perley Creek, Ellison Creek (plus small side \), Myrtle Creek

The **East Verde River** is a true Mogollon Rim stream, forming between Highview and Immigrant points at over 7000 feet and flowing down into the Verde gorge 42 miles away. Once grazed hard, the river and its watershed are now in better-than-average condition. Knotgrass and young willows crowd at the water's edge; moss, ferns, columbines, raspberries, all adorn the streambanks up under the rim, while sycamore and Fremont cottonwood groves provide shade in the lower canyon. The headwaters are scalloped under the steepest, most spectacular portion of the Rim, shared with the Tonto Creek headwaters spreading immediately to the east. These two upper watersheds contain nearly all of the icy, step-across trout waters falling off the Rim's southern edge—here the drop is 2500 feet, in as little as three or four miles. The first 1000 feet, of course, is nearly vertical. No other streams in the state are like them. They arise from limestone springs, flow from one to three steep miles in lush shade, then disappear under the ground in the dry, pine savannas away from the Rim's temperature shadow. If you were to take the combined flow of all the little under-the-rim rills of the East Verde watershed, you could certainly account for more than the stream's 29 cfs of flow.

Though the East Verde is not much more than a fair-sized creek, it has more water than by rights it should. The stream mechanics of many Arizona watersheds are quite peculiar, owing to the state's overall water scarcity. For instance, neighboring Verde River tributary Fossil Creek sees its flow reduced in its first quarter mile below the huge Fossil Springs from 45 cfs to 0.2 cfs by the Arizona Public Service Company, which has cut a flume for the displaced water into the south wall of the Fossil Canyon, feeding a decrepit but still functioning mini-hydro plant far below. East Verde is transformed right under the rim in just the opposite way, from a crystal-clear headwater spring creek with a 2-6 cfs late-summer flow to a major water source, by a diversion over the divide from the little Colorado watershed at Blue Ridge Reservoir, formed by a dam on East Clear Creek. This is a payback by the Phelps Dodge Copper Corporation, which built the reservoir, for water taken from the Black River and pumped over another divide into Eagle Creek, a Gila River tributary, where it feeds PD's mammoth Morenci mining operation.

The extra boost of water for East Verde is a mixed blessing—very cold, around 50 degrees in the summer months, but also often turbid, due to watershed problems over the divide, filling the limestone cobble of East Verde with a layer of fine, orange-brown silt which hampers natural trout reproduction. Heavy stockings counteract this, and the extra-cold water makes for some trout fishing all the way into the deserts of the Mazatzal Wilderness, with a few strays finding their way even to the river's mouth at the Verde mainstem. Under the rim the stream is a heavily-used but also heavily-stocked. Stream-bred browns are scattered about and tend to survive farther downstream; the uppermost reaches hold wild rainbows, all the way up to the Piper-Pierson springs. Below State 87 smallmouth bass start to appear, the trout seeking the deeper pools below fast water.

Near the very head of the East Verde, the remains of the old Piper state fish hatchery can be found. This was the major source for the state's planted trout until 1937, when a new facility was built on the upper Tonto. This uppermost mile to two miles of the East Verde, the part above the Phelps Dodge inflow, is still the best, with some wild rainbows showing the coloration of Apache hybrids—how this came about is not clear. Access

EAST VERDE DRAINAGE

to the upper reaches of the stream is good east of AZ 87, the main route from Phoenix up and over the rim, either by the Control Road (FR 64) or the Houston Mesa Road (FR 199), which follows the East Verde up to the Highline National Recreation Trail (FT 31) just a couple of miles below the rim.

Many of the East Verde's tributaries are themselves fly-fishing destinations, for hikers and backpackers. These are amazing streams, flowing like tiny, ice-cold mirages through oak, pine, and manzanita before disappearing beneath the ground. The Control Road finds all of them dry, but if you hike to the very head of each dry bed, you find limestone outcroppings, springs, and wild trout. Both the East Verde and its micro-tributaries can be readily fished by the Highline Trail (FT 31), a Forest Service pathway that follows the base of the Mogollon Rim for 50 total miles from the hamlet of Pine to AZ 260 near Colcord Road junction. Pristine **Pine Creek** is a giant among the tributaries, a fair-sized, plunging stream of roughly 1 cfs minimum and 4 cfs average flow, passing through deep green woods over a mossy, rocky bed. In upper reaches its water never exceeds 62 degrees. Water pennies abound. It holds browns and rainbows in its uppermost 4 miles from the rim to Pine village, where it is now pumped dry. Water re-emerges in a hot canyon below the village, three miles or so above Tonto Natural Bridge State Park. At the bridge, ice-cold limestone springs form falls spilling into travertine pools, where visitors crowd above and below to watch. A few trout have found their way here, but mainly stunted green sunfish make do in the 60-degree water. Some other wild trout have made their way into the very lowest part of the stream by ascending from the confluence with the East Verde River. Though permanent flow is spotty below its first four miles, this stream is highly productive, with fish mass of 15 grams/square meter of streambed in the headwaters, over twice the average rate for streams in the Rocky Mountains and northern Colorado Plateau.

Immediately to the east, uppermost **Webber Creek** flows through a green Eden of alder trees, wild grape, raspberry, thimbleberry, and other *Rubus* tangles, woodbine, yellow columbine, and mossy boulders. Near its head it is a fine little trout stream, holding rainbows in its upper 4 1/2 miles above the Highline Trail crossing. Below the trail the fishing is a bit spottier, before the stream dries up about a mile and a half above the Control Road. A spur road (FR 440) accesses a bit of this lowermost fishing.

A bit farther east, the truly tiny streams begin. **Bray** and **Sycamore creeks** are ice-cold trickles with occasional brook trout and rainbows. **Chase Creek** for many years provided water for a private trout hatchery, now the site of a Girl Scout camp—it's dry below the fence. These waters have been stocked privately in the past. Accessible from above by the Highline Trail, all three are at least worth a look.

Jump-across **Dude Creek** has .25 cfs yearly minimum, 1 cfs yearly average flow. It used to hold brookies, also, but all fish in the stream died after the June 1990 Dude Fire, which cleared 24,000 acres along the Rim and also killed six firefighters on a work-release program from the Arizona prison system. No trout have managed to return since. The Gila Trout Recovery Team is now preparing to re-introduce Gila trout here.

Bonita Creek is a bit larger, holding .7 cfs minimum, 3.5 cfs average flow. Its water ranges from 55 to 64 degrees during a typical 24-hour cycle in June—good enough for 3 miles of habitat for a wild population of rainbows. It too is recovering from the Dude Fire, and some rainbows have returned here. **Perley Creek**, another tiny, is the next stream along the Rim. Unaffected by the fire, it still holds a surprising number of rainbow trout way up. **Ellison Creek,** five to six feet wide, has .2 cfs minimum and somewhat less than 1 cfs yearly average flow of cold, pure water in its upper reaches. Like Pine Creek, it seldom if ever exceeded 62 degrees before the fire, and has a side branch under Myrtle Point on the Rim. This system was also blasted by the Dude Fire and has yet to stabilize. Very few trout have returned to date. Heavy rains are still bringing mud and rockslides down into the channel. This creek may one day hold Gila trout, also.

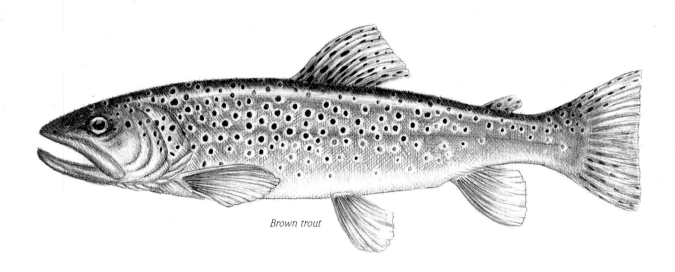

Brown trout

5. East Clear Creek System

Name:	East Clear Creek
Location:	Coconino National Forest
Maps:	Coconino NF Visitors Map, USGS 1:100,000 series, Sedona edition
Elevation:	7000-3900 feet
Average Volume:	83 cfs near Willow Creek Confluence; flows vary greatly and may drop well below 5 cfs in dry months.
Length of Fishing Water:	95 miles
Best Times:	April, May, September-November
Fish Species:	Brown trout, rainbow trout, flannelmouth sucker, bluehead sucker, speckled dace, Little Colorado spinedace, golden shiner, fathead minnow
Tributaries:	Miller Canyon, East Fork Miller Canyon, Barbershop Canyon, General Springs Canyon, Leonard Canyon, East Fork Leonard Canyon, West Fork Leonard Canyon, Dane Canyon, Merritt Draw Canyon, Willow Creek, Open Draw, Gentry Canyon, Turkey Creek, Beaver Creek, Bear Canyon

Northeast-flowing **East Clear Creek** is a beautiful canyon stream, the main permanent tributary of the Little Colorado River, representing the only major trout-bearing watershed flowing northwards off the 200-mile-long Mogollon Mesa. Aside from the White Mountain drainages, this system also contains the most significant collective trout habitat in the state. Though impacted in recent years by heavy logging, nearly 100 miles of its once-clear mainstem contain at least some brown or rainbow trout, while the upper tributary reaches above 7000 feet also support brook char.

East Clear Creek's canyon dips further into the Mogollon rock strata as it cuts first across, then down the Mogollon Mesa. Acquiring its flow from tributaries 6 to 7 miles above Blue Ridge Reservoir, it first exposes the volcanic basalt that tops the whole plateau, then sedimentary gravel conglomerates, then the same colorful sandstones, the Kaibab limestone and Toroweap formation that visitors admire from Canyon village and the south rim of the Grand Canyon. Water is drawn from the system via big pumps at U-shaped **Blue Ridge Reservoir** (70 acres, 6720 feet), at the junction of two twisting, narrow canyons. You can barely climb down to the water, especially when it is drawn down twenty or more feet, except at a long, narrow boat ramp, and you need a boat to fish successfully, with motors up to 8 hp allowed. Large rainbow and brown trout are (stuck) here. The water is often murky, and algae blooms can be noted in summer. The ridge is blue, the water is not. A campground above Rock Crossing overlooks the lake and is reachable from AZ 87 and FR 751.

In the lower reaches of the canyon the color bands of the rock strata rise directly up on either side of the twisting, meandering streambed. Viewed from above, the canyon looks like a set of interlocking, rounded cliffs. White and Douglas fir and ponderosa pines line the clifftops and wandering ridges in the upper 20 miles of the stream. Along the canyon bottom, down to 5000 feet, are gray alders, narrowleaf cottonwoods, boxelder trees, black locusts, and Arizona walnuts. FR 137 at Mack's Crossing gets you into the middle reaches where the better fishing begins, FR 211 and FR 95 get you into the upper, coldwater canyon where trout dominate, provided there's enough water for them. The browns can be caught in the evenings with nymphs.

Below the confluence of Leonard Canyon the country opens up, giving rise to three or four species of the dull-colored juniper trees. Grama grass prairies appear in the drier, lower slopes near and beyond the Coconino and Sitgreaves forest boundaries. For its last forty miles or so, East Clear is a high desert stream, its bottom still filled with remnants of a gallery cottonwood-willow forest. There is some flow throughout the canyon at all seasons of the year, but in drier months you'll find intermittent dry reaches. At the lowermost end of the stream, East Clear Creek Canyon is dammed at 5000 feet to form narrow, twisting 60-acre **Clear Creek Reservoir**, with (a few) rainbow trout and bass.

East Clear has a classic "dendritic" (Gr. *dendron*, "tree"), or branching, drainage pattern, its many tributaries similar to western Pennsylvania's streams, or the trout waters of southwestern Wisconsin's Driftless Zone. Its upper tributaries start with **Miller Canyon** and its **East Fork**, both wild rainbow fisheries of a sort. Grassy-banked and filled with dace, the streams provide a few rainbows every quarter mile or so in the deeper holes. **General Springs Creek** adds 6 miles of similar water. **Bear Canyon Creek** adds 2 1/2 miles of flow and slightly better fishing. **Barbershop** and its tributary **Dane Canyon**, 16 and 8 miles respectively, are also better fisheries, with brown and rainbow trout in the lower stream reaches and a few brook char in the upper end. **Merritt Draw**, 2 miles, drains into upper Barbershop.

Leonard Canyon provides 23 miles of fair to poor habitat for wild rainbow trout, plus smaller numbers of browns, with brook char in the upper reaches. Golden shiners and fathead minnows, originally left behind by bait fishermen, are now naturalized; they form a prey base for some of the larger trout. The canyon passes through ancient Kaibab limestone sediments below 7340-foot, 55-acre **Knoll Lake,** a generally unproductive rainbow trout impoundment. Leonard Canyon is mostly a high-elevation stream, passing through mixed conifer, Gambel oak, and ponderosa woodland; at the canyon bottom is a vigorous deciduous gallery of boxelder, gray (thinleaf) alder, Arizona walnut, Rocky Mountain maple, and many willows. Only at its entry into East Clear Creek at 6400 feet do junipers start to show on the slopes above Leonard Canyon. Few cattle find their way into the canyon bottom, and even fewer people. This stream is also crowded with several small tributaries in its upper reaches: **West Leonard Canyon** has 6 to 7 miles of wild rainbow trout habitat. **East Leonard Canyon**, 2 to 3 miles long, provides wild rainbows. **Buck Springs Canyon**, 5 1/2 miles, empties into upper Leonard nearby. **Middle Leonard** drains Lost Lake right on the edge of the Rim, all rainbow trout water.

Just to the east, **Willow Creek** is a much drier watercourse of 26 miles, holding some water in scattered pools and a very few wild browns, as well as rainbows. This stream once held fair numbers of trout, but, today, if you follow its course, expect to do a great deal more walking than fishing. There are also a few trout in **Open Draw**, fewer yet in **Gentry Canyon, Turkey Creek,** and **Beaver Canyon.** These sub-drainages closely resemble the upper Leonard Canyon tributaries, except there is less water, for some reason, and far fewer fish. All these streams subside during dry periods, becoming a collection of occasional brief flows and hidden pools, where you can find an occasional trout.

Bear Canyon, the highest, most reliable tributary to Willow Creek, holds wild brook char in 5 miles of water below 7600-foot, 60-acre **Bear Canyon Lake.** Rainbows are in the lake, plus a very few brookies and even a few arctic grayling, which don't seem to mind the late-summer algae "blooms." Special regulations allow artificial lures only, which means fewer empty salmon egg jars, and less litter, also fewer fishermen. There is a short, steep trail to lakeside, but no road. Boats with or without electric motors are allowed. No gasoline.

6. CHEVELON CREEK SYSTEM

Name: Chevelon Canyon
Location: Sitgreaves National Forest
Maps: Apache-Sitgreaves National Forest Visitors Map, USGS 1:100,000 series, Showlow edition
Elevation: 7000-3900 feet
Average Flow: 5 cfs
Length: 83 miles
Best Times: April, May, September-November
Fish Species: Rainbow trout, brook char, brown trout, Little Colorado spinedace, common carp, bluehead sucker, red shiner, golden shiner
Tributaries: West Fork Chevelon, Willow Springs, Woods, Wildcat, and Black Canyons

Chevelon Canyon, named for a cowboy who died after eating poisonous plants, starts at 7200 feet and flows gently northwards across the top of the Mogollon Plateau for 100 miles before emptying into the Little Colorado River 25 miles below Holbrook. Its headwater reaches are shaded by north slope white and Douglas fir, ponderosa, and some Southwestern white pine and Gambel oak, with streambank mountain-lover, the bottoms also filled with gray alder, boxelder, narrowleaf cottonwood, even Arizona walnut. As the canyon moves to the lower, northern end of the Plateau, piñon pine and alligator juniper start to appear, with cliffrose and grama grasses filling the open slopes.

Chevelon's narrow, closed-in canyon is not really deep, especially compared to the rugged watercourses below the rim, but its smooth-edged sandstone-limestone rimrock makes climbing down to the stream and climbing out again surprisingly difficult. The whole canyon is far less visited than any of the major waters below the rim. You get the impression of being in real wilderness once you're down in the canyon, and in fact it is much more remote than it would seem at first. One access is the Telephone Trail (#103) off FR 169 and Fr 119, built for a former single-strand telephone line. This trail gets you into the canyon, seven miles north of Chevelon's source, but doesn't lead back out. Upper Chevelon, like Woods Canyon, is intermittent, with the trout scattered in permanent pockets of water. The best fishing is below Horsetrap Canyon and above Canyon Lake, where the water is cold and the flow reliable, but trout can be found farther downstream. You'll find wild browns in the middle portions of this 80-plus-mile stream, down to the boundary of the Apache-Sitgreaves National Forest. Occasionally, some reach 20 inches or more. Brookies are found way upstream in the headwaters, along with a good share of rainbows near and below Chevelon Canyon Lake. There only real road crossing of the canyon, Chevelon Crossing at FR 504 near the Sitgreaves National Forest boundary, roughly marks the downstream end of Chevelon as a coldwater fishery. Below the forest, the stream sinks underground periodically, finally emerging on Hopi Indian lands near Winslow, Arizona, where it supports a bewildering array of native and exotic warmwater fishes, but no trout or bass.

Lightly-fished **Chevelon Canyon Lake**, 175 acres at 6400 feet, is hidden at the bottom of the Chevelon Canyon, and accessible on foot only via a deteriorated and abandoned one-mile road. The lake is managed as a "Blue Ribbon" rainbow fishery by AZ G&F. Small motors (up to 8 hp,) are allowed, if you want to lug them out of the canyon along with your boat. Locals not wishing to "pack it in, pack it out" chain a few small boats to trees along the shore, and carry only their motors. Golden shiner baitfish allow browns and rainbows to grow big here—up to

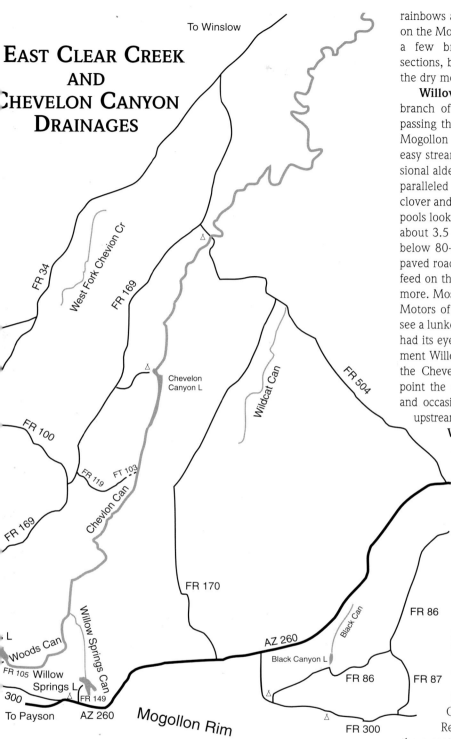

EAST CLEAR CREEK
AND
CHEVELON CANYON
DRAINAGES

To Winslow

FR 34

West Fork Chevlon Cr

FR 169

Chevelon Canyon L

Wildcat Can

FR 504

FR 100

FR 119   FT 103

FR 169

Chevlon Can

FR 170

FR 86

Black Can

AZ 260

Black Canyon L

FR 86   FR 87

Woods Can

Willow Springs Can

FR 105 Willow Springs L

FR 149

300

To Payson   AZ 260

Mogollon Rim

FR 300

rainbows at 7500 feet. Above the lake, the first one ever "built" on the Mogollon Plateau, is tiny **East Fork Woods Canyon** with a few brookies. Woods Canyon proper is dry in some sections, but occasional beaver ponds will allow trout to survive the dry months.

Willow Springs Canyon, the other, even smaller headwater branch of Chevelon, is a slowly meandering meadow stream passing through remnants of tall timber on the very top of the Mogollon Plateau, with a few waist-deep, still pools. This is an easy stream to follow, since very few willows and only an occasional alder clump block your way, and, easier yet, the stream is paralleled by an old logging tote road, now overgrown with clover and bunchgrasses. Though the water is amber-colored, the pools look good, holding well-fed brook char, some very large, in about 3.5 miles of hard-pressed beaver habitat. The creek flows below 80-acre, 7500-foot **Willow Springs Lake**, accessible by paved road and stocked with rainbows and browns. The browns feed on their share of golden shiners and reach seven pounds or more. Most trout pulled out are from recent plantings, however. Motors of up to 8 horsepower are permitted. Sometimes you'll see a lunker brown that has died of old age wash up on shore and had its eyes and gills pecked at by the birds. Below this impoundment Willow Springs Canyon meets with Woods Canyon to form the Chevelon, where the canyon narrows considerably. At this point the creek becomes intermittent, with rockslides, deadfalls, and occasional trout pools replacing the ferns and sedges found upstream.

West Fork Chevelon Creek, usually dry at its mouth, is a sometimes stream, worth exploring in wet years, iffy in dry. It holds browns in occasional pools scattered over 8 to 9 miles of streambed; the whole stream is mostly dry in the dry months. **Wildcat Canyon** is by all accounts another ephemeral stream, mostly a dry bed in summer, and certainly not on anyone's list of trout waters. Even so, streams like Wildcat and West Fork Chevelon do have a subsurface flow (in Arizona people often speak of streams flowing "underground"), and very occasionally you can find a bend in the canyon where this always-cold water seeps into and out of a deep standing pool. Sometimes, especially in wet years, there will be a number of trout in one of these holes, and not always small ones either. Finding such a place is always a fascinating possibility, at least for me. The trout seem to ascend each canyon from its respective confluence with Chevelon Creek, near the Sitgreaves Forest boundary. Rest assured that few if any people will have fished one of these spots in a long, long while, if you can find one. The same can be said of neighboring **Black Canyon**, which is dammed at 7560 feet near its head, to form sea-green **Black Canyon Lake**, 78 acres and stocked heavily with rainbows. Chances of finding fish in Black Canyon below the dam are smaller, however—it meets Chevelon way down in the desert southwest of Holbrook and so Chevelon fish have a harder time exploring its lower end. For that matter, don't go off expecting to find trout in any of these three streams—at least not in your first few outings. Ask a local about trout fishing in one of these canyons and he'll most likely scoff at the idea.

14 pounds, with better fishing early and late in the year. Spring rainbow runs and reproduction occur above the lake, and many rainbows are also stocked in the stream itself at Durfee Crossing seven miles below.

Woods Canyon Creek is one of the two brook char headwater branches of Chevelon Canyon, wandering along the rim for about 6 miles below the spillway of 55-acre, aspen-ringed **Woods Canyon Lake**, with store and campground and stocked with

7. TONTO CREEK SYSTEM

Name: Tonto Creek
Location: Tonto National Forest, Apache and Graham Counties, Arizona
Maps: Tonto NF Visitors Map, USGS 1:100,000 Series, Payson edition
Elevation: 7000-3900 feet
Average Volume: 30 cfs
Length of Trout Water: 32 miles (Total stream length is 63 miles.)
Best Times: March-May, October-November
Fish Species: Brown trout, rainbow trout, Sonoran sucker, longfin dace, green sunfish
Tributaries: Upper forks, Dick Williams Creek, Horton Creek, Christopher Creek, Hunter Creek, Sharp Creek, Gordon Canyon Creek, Haigler Creek, Marsh Creek, Spring Creek, Houston Creek

The name **Tonto Creek** is synonymous with the Mogollon Rim, called the "Tonto Rim" by Zane Grey who spent idyllic summers in a cabin he built just off the old Highline Trail a half mile or so from the creek's headwaters Here he cranked out five of his western allegories, including the title *Under the Tonto Rim*. Though better known for his catches of giant marlin of the south seas or steelhead from North Umpqua and Rogue Rivers, Grey often hiked the trails near his cabin, looking for turkey or bear with his son Romer or carrying his fly rod to fish the Tonto and neighboring streams. Today upper Tonto Creek is crowded with tourists, but the pools are nearly the same as those Zane Grey fished. The whole length of the Tonto is still undammed, much of its middle and lower reaches still wild and unreachable by any road. This is hands down the southwest's most famous trout stream, and

though small it is still perhaps one of the best streams for its size in the state.

Trout fishing on the Tonto begins above the tiny settlement of Gisela, and its upper drainage contains several excellent tributaries. As with most other streams flowing south of the rim, the Tonto's shaded lower canyon was once filled with groves of towering broadleaf trees, marshes, and almost impenetrable willow and alder thickets. The clearing of these forests near the turn of the century, both for firewood and as leafy emergency cattle feed, coupled with heavy cattle grazing, stripped both Tonto Creek and the grassy mesas above of nearly all protective vegetation, and subsequent floods in the early 1900s tore out much of the lower streambed. To protect the Salt watershed against such ravages was the primary reason for establishing the Tonto National Forest in 1901.

Today, the lower end of Tonto Creek is hot and muddy in the summer, swelling like a flooded desert wash after each rainstorm. Upstream from the old cattle ranges beginning at Gisela, the roads disappear, water clears, and trout can be found in increasing numbers up to the mouth of Haigler Creek, in aptly named Hellsgate Canyon. The Arizona Highway 260 bridge roughly marks the change of the Tonto from a tourist destination to a wild backpacking/flyfishing haven. The narrow Hellsgate Section of the stream, begins just below Bear Flat 4 miles south of AZ 260, and the deep

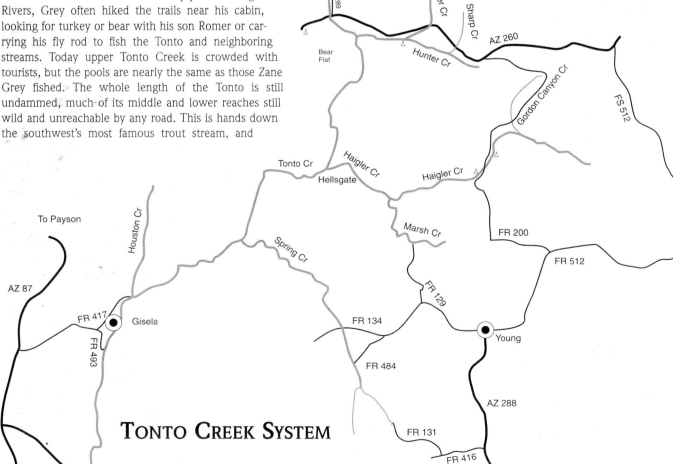

TONTO CREEK SYSTEM

canyon itself ends just above Gisela. This stretch is becoming more popular every year with canyoneers straying south from the increasingly crowded slot canyons of southern Utah. Few of these adventurers fish, but you might greet a party or two if you decide to make the 35-mile wade/hike/descent from Bear Flat to Gisela. The canyon is cold, the desert above hot. Some of the deepest pools in this canyon approach 30 feet. Who knows what monsters lie at the bottom? Elsewhere along the canyon, browns and rainbows over twenty inches can be seen through the clear water, lurking in the bottoms of some of the smaller pools. These are very difficult to arouse from a seeming collective slumber, yet occasionally one can be made to move: An acquaintance once hooked a struggling 12-inch trout, only to see a 25-incher arise from the bottom and devour it. In the lower reaches of this section towards Gisela, where it opens a bit, you see desert vegetation on the slopes above— including agave plants, even saguaro cactus—and 20-inch trout in the pools below. Where else but the Southwest?

Above Hellsgate a number of headwater tributaries enter. The fishing in these is surprisingly good, as it is on the Tonto itself above the highway bridge, where it is paralleled by a good forest road all the way to its source directly under the Mogollon Rim. Here Tonto Spring wells up at 7500 feet, the site of the recently-renovated *grande dame* of Arizona fish hatcheries. The hatchery raises rainbows, gathered from broodstock purchased from other states, about 130,000 per year, mostly for lakes north of the Mogollon Rim. Wild browns thrive in the stream's clear water from here down to the AZ 260 bridge, supplemented by at least weekly plantings of rainbows. This arrangement keeps both serious and casual anglers happy, for the most part. Surrounded by upland shrubs and grasses surging up through the blackened snags of the Dude Fire, the unaffected, unburned stream bottom is still smothered by greenery, from blackberry tangles and raspberry shrubs to sycamore and Douglas fir groves. Tiny, overlooked **Dick Williams Creek** is a drink of water entering a mile below the hatchery, where trout sometimes stray. **Horton Creek** has a low-water flow of about 1.6 cfs and contains 7 to 8 miles of water below the Rim, ranging from 7000 down to 5400 feet. Water temperatures here generally do not exceed 67 degrees in summer. Not stocked, holding stray rainbows and wild browns, it must be hiked and offers comparative solitude in 2.5 miles of stream. Its mouth is usually dry, the first fish found about a half mile up from the Tonto. Immediately below Horton, limestone-filled **Big Canyon** offers permanent flow and a very occasional trout in its lowermost half mile or so. **Christopher Creek**, 3 to 5 cfs, enters below the main highway, AZ 260. It is heavily stocked with rainbow trout, holds many small wild browns in its lower end, and has a very rugged little box called See Canyon farther upstream, where the fish are larger and few people venture. Fishermen are well rewarded here. The headwaters are cold, but the lower end sees 70-degree temperatures by early June, ending the rainbow plants at Christopher Creek campground, but also providing crowd relief for the more serious fisherman. The crowds and rock music subside, but the wild brown trout remain in the murky brown pools on the stream's lower end. Christopher Creek tributary **Hunter Creek** parallels AZ 260 but is out of sight and somewhat hard to reach.

Joining Christopher from the south, right at that stream's namesake campground, it has 2.5 miles of wild rainbow water in its upper end, but few or no trout in its lower end, where deep, stagnant pools provide ideal summer conditions for green sunfish of up to 10 inches. Sub-tributary **Sharp Creek** provides refuge for a very occasional trout near its mouth into Hunter.

Way downstream within the Hellsgate Wilderness, the Tonto meets **Haigler Creek**. This stream holds stocker rainbows in the campground and roadside areas under Naegelin Rim, near its source, and wild browns below for 15 or so total miles. This is a good-sized, major stream of 15-20 cfs, nearly the size of Tonto itself. Access to the upper Haigler is easy via Young Road, through true cattle country. Grasslands along the benches are cropped to the ground, and the water in the stream below is frequently discolored. FR 291 leaves AZ 260 east of Christopher Creek. This skirts the headwaters of the major Haigler sub-tributary, **Gordon Canyon Creek,** which has 10 to 11 miles of flow and wild rainbows. Winding around Turkey Peak, the road re-joins then roughly parallels Haigler Creek for 4 miles or so before heading over to Young. The lower section of Haigler Creek descends into Hellsgate Canyon and is just as deep and rugged as the Tonto mainstem. To get here you have to descend along the Creek, in the process passing virtually unfished south sub-tributary **Marsh Creek,** which has wild browns.

Spring Creek, small (2 cfs average) but pristine, enters Tonto from the south, draining the north end of the straight-up Sierra Ancha Mountains. As a trout habitat it is long and wild—8 miles of prime water for wild browns in its uppermost course, with at least some trout for the remainder of its 20-mile total length. The stream also contains a significant population of native warmwater species, particularly roundtail chubs. The stream banks are in excellent condition, with vigorous growth of alder, boxelder, Bonpland willow, and Arizona sycamore shading many deep pools, and undercut banks holding surprising numbers of fish—some of them brown trout 15 or more inches in length. Wading sandals and backpacking gear are the equipment you'll need to find these trout. The 12-mile road access to the old Flying W Ranch via FR 129 and FR 134 west of Young is rough going, with the last couple of miles suitable only for high-clearance trucks or utility vehicles. From this crossing you can hike ten miles downstream through a narrow but passable valley, before climbing down through a gorge which could well be named Hellsgate, Jr., into the Tonto confluence within Hellsgate Wilderness. There is an equally rough spur departing from FR 134 at Mailbox Mesa, FR 484, which meets the creek below looming Cline Mesa a couple of miles upstream from Flying W. From here you can wade some ten miles upstream through narrows, deep shade, and summertime columbines to the headwaters, which can also be reached via FS 131. This last road, to the old Spring Creek Ranch, meets the AZ 288 ten miles south of Young. Once you're on the stream, your chances of seeing other hikers are minimal, far less than on the Tonto.

The lowermost trout stream to enter the Tonto, **Houston Creek** flows southward, arising from springs in the Star Valley and entering the Tonto in the desert just above Gisela, AZ. It has 6 miles of wild brown trout water.

8. THE SIERRA ANCHAS: SALOME AND CHERRY CREEKS

Name: Salome Creek
Location: Salome Wilderness, Tonto National Forest, Apache and Graham Counties, Arizona,
Elevation: 7000-3900 feet, coldwater reach
Average Volume: 4 cfs
Length of fishing water: 22 miles
Best Times: April, May, September-November
Fish Species: Brown trout, rainbow trout, roundtail chub
Tributaries: Reynolds Creek, McFadden Creek, Rose Creek, Workman Creek

Salome Creek falls into Roosevelt Lake midway between Tonto and Cherry Creeks. Though it parallels these larger streams, it doesn't reach all the way to the Mogollon Rim, forming on 7500-foot McFadden Peak thirty miles to the south and draining the west slope of the rugged Sierra Ancha Mountains. This is a much smaller watershed than the Tonto and it accumulates far less water. Most of Salome Creek is a roadless and trail-less desert canyon, much of it within the Tonto National Forest's Salome Wilderness. A few trout are in the upper reaches of Salome Canyon, including wild browns, and some wander far downstream in

THE SIERRA ANCHAS: SALOME AND CHERRY CREEKS

cooler months, where they hole up. A fall fishing/backpacking trip is the best way to appreciate this small stream. Here is as far down into the desert as you will ever find wild trout.

Upper tributaries **Workman, McFadden, Rose,** and **Reynolds creeks** provide most of the water for Salome. All hold trout at least occasionally, Workman almost always. The Anchas, a companion range to the troutless Mazatzal Mountains immediately to the west, are an amazing micro-habitat stretching nearly straight above the eastern end of Lake Roosevelt. Here, genuine Sonoran desert yields to shade-filled groves of Douglas fir, ponderosa pine, and Gambel oak. The cobbled stream bottoms are filled with tree-sized alders, low-lying willow thickets, and spreading sycamores. Almost all the fishing practiced here is of the roadside variety, with summertime anglers following the Workman and Reynolds Creek plants along spur roads FR 487 and 410, but there is much more fishing available to those who want to invest a little more in the way of time and shoe leather. As a rule, the trout tend to wander below this roadside area, down into the canyon below the joining of Reynolds and Workman. Generally, you will need to fish either with a handful of Phoenicians for the stockers at Workman Falls off FR 487 when the water is high, or else all by yourself farther downstream in the fall, below the Young Road (AZ 288), which crosses both Workman and Reynolds creeks. Don't be surprised to find all of these tributaries dried out and filled with bleached white stones late in the year. During such dry periods, the trout find hidden puddles in places where the streams are forced between rock outcroppings or below small, ice-cold seeps. These reaches are scarce, indeed, but once you've found them catching the trout is all too easy—even with a cumbersome fly rod.

Three miles below the place where McFadden, Workman, and Reynolds creeks join together, **Salome Creek** proper begins and the canyon deepens considerably. In some sections you can touch the opposing canyon walls with outstretched hands. Here the wild browns start to appear, as well as the odd rainbow washed down from above, plus roundtail chubs and other warmwater species. A few trout are scattered upstream, also, as far as Turkey Creek mouth six or so miles above Workman Creek mouth. Wading in and out of the water is the only way to go. In fall, expect to find good fishing in the deeper pools but also scattered dry pockets where the flow of the stream goes under the gravel and stony debris. In wetter weather, the going is a little tougher and, needless to say, in July and August heavy thunder showers can make the Hell's Hole section at the Salome Wilderness boundary really dangerous. Some waterfalls approach thirty feet. If you want to give yourself four to six days in the fall, you can fish all the way down to FR 60, just above Roosevelt Lake. Narrows provide plenty of hiding places for the angler and opportunities to cast for the larger trout without being seen, even while proceeding downstream. The five miles above FR 60 are more level, the canyon widens a bit, and the fish are harder to find.

All in all, the Salome is not classic water by any stretch of the imagination, but that's the whole attraction here. Catching wild trout, an essentially Arctic and sub-arctic family of fish, from an icy stream flowing through a slot canyon in exotic Southwest desert mountains is an experience not soon forgotten. You've probably not ever done that, and almost surely not been at Salome Creek Canyon to do it.

CHERRY CREEK

Name:	Cherry Creek
Location:	Tonto National Forest, Apache and Graham Counties, Arizona
Maps:	Tonto National Forest Visitors Map, USGS 1:100,000 series, Payson
Elevation:	5600-2600 feet
Average Volume:	10 cfs (above Ellison Ranch)
Length of Trout Water:	47 miles (total stream length 52 miles)
Best Times:	April, May, September-November
Fish Species:	Brown trout, rainbow trout, Sonoran sucker, longfin dace, roundtail chub, desert sucker, speckled dace, green sunfish, smallmouth bass, yellow bullhead
Tributaries:	Pueblo Canyon Creek

Cherry Creek is the major stream of the Sierra Anchas, nearly 50 miles of trout water of widely varying quality draining the precipitous eastern end of the range. It begins above Naegelin Rim, a brief extension of Mogollon Mesa, just west of the Fort Apache Reservation then flows south, finally draining into the Salt River at 2500 feet within the Salt River Canyon Wilderness, 10 to 15 miles above Roosevelt Lake. Most of the spectacular lower stream flows through a hole in the mountains and is hard to get to. The upper reach is accessible from the backwoods town of Young, Arizona, reachable via AZ 288 from Globe, a part-paved, part-graded road that connects with the Apache Trail (AZ 88) and zigzags through the other side of the Sierra Anchas. A jeep track (FR 203) parallels the upper reaches of the creek, passing through a supposed federal wilderness area. Young lies just above Cherry Creek's west bank in a little basin called Pleasant Valley, site of the Tewksberry range war in the 1870s, something akin to the Hatfield-McCoy feud in West Virginia. Hatfields feuded over a pig, Tewksberrys over a cow. Feuds continue today. This was and is cattle country— too much so, as far as the fishery in Cherry Creek is concerned.

Above Young, Cherry Creek is mostly ephemeral but does contain a few trout under the Naegelin Rim. Below Young, the stream starts to descend into an astonishing canyon. It is close to 4000 feet from the streambed to the top of the Sierra Anchas looming almost directly overhead. Rainbows can be found as far as 10 miles below Young, with browns holing up farther downstream, directly under the Sierra Anchas. This section of the stream is flooded regularly due to overgrazing on the rangelands above the canyon, and scoured nearly clean due to the narrowness of the canyon walls. Water levels fluctuate, and fishing is marginal. The wild brown trout that inhabit this stream fare very poorly under these conditions. The floods decimate the browns here as elsewhere in the Southwest, but have far less effect on native species such as the endangered razorback sucker which still finds a home here.

Like West Clear Creek to the north, Cherry Creek itself lies in a peculiar double canyon. The outer canyon is formed by the mountains, the Anchas on the west, looming up to 7700 feet, and Pendleton, Vosberg and other mesas directly to the east. The inner canyon is a narrow slot cut more recently by the creek waters, only three to four hundred feet deep, as opposed to the three- to four-thousand-foot depth of the outer canyon. A rough road (FR 203) follows above the inner canyon, invisible and inaccessible to someone on the water, but visible far below as a tiny thread to someone looking down from the Anchas.

As the Cherry Creek Canyon passes below the Anchas and nears the Salt River in the desert, it opens up, the stream braiding out into gravel bars and shallows lined by velvet mesquite and burro brush. The fishing suffers more here than it does above, but a precious few browns can still be found down nearly to the 3000-foot level. These are small, generally. The brown's life expectancy is low in Cherry Creek, due to floods. Improvement in this state of affairs seems to be on the way as the U. S. Forest Service finds itself gradually forced to limit cattle activity on Southwestern streams. The U.S. Fish and Wildlife Service has recently proposed Cherry Creek as critical habitat for the endangered razorback sucker. Such actions force an accounting for riparian and watershed damage caused by the livestock.

The side canyons of Cherry Creek from the west fall down from the precipitous east face of the Sierra Ancha range and are almost impassable to cattle. As a result, there are a few coldwater streams with higher-quality flow and streamside vegetation far more lush than that of the main canyon. **Pueblo Canyon Creek**, one of these, holds dace and possibly a few trout, as does neighboring **PB Creek**. Streams like these are inspected by the state game and fish once every ten to twenty years, and by adventurous fishermen only slightly more often.

DÜRTEN KAMPMANN

9. CANYON, CIBECUE, AND CARRIZO CREEK SYSTEMS

Name: Canyon Creek
Location: Tonto National Forest, Fort Apache Indian Reservation,

Elevation: 7500-3100 feet
Length of Fishing Water: 48 miles
Best Times: April, May, September-November
Fish Species: Brown trout, rainbow trout, desert sucker, speckled dace
Tributaries: Mule Creek, Swamp Creek, Rotten Spring Creek

Mogollon Rim

AZ 260
FR 300
IR33
OW Cr
FR 33
FR34
Mule Cr
FR 188
IR34
White Spring
Canyon Cr
FR 512
FR 358
Rotten Spring Cr
CT Spring
Salt Cr
Cibeque Cr
IR34
Mud Cr
IR 35
FR202
Carrizo Cr
IR12
IR12
Cibecue
Canyon Cr
IR12
IR30
Spring Cr
Cibeque Cr
US 60
Salt River
To Globe

CANYON, CIBECUE, AND CARRIZO CREEKS

Canyon Creek springs to life full-grown, right under the Mogollon Rim in the Tonto National Forest. Then it flows due south towards the Salt River through some of the most remote country in Arizona, reaching the Salt some 48 miles downstream. The lowermost ten miles, seldom visited by humans, passes beneath a sheer eastern wall which earns Canyon Creek its name, even in this land of many canyons. Most of the stream lies within the nearly roadless western edge of the Fort Apache Indian Reservation, where a tribal permit gives you the opportunity to hike cross-country then down into the canyon, fishing for as far or as long as you wish. No trail here, except the canyon itself. The permits are necessary and available in Whiteriver, Hondah, and Reservation Lake, plus several Arizona towns off the reservation, such as Springerville, Showlow, Pinetop, Mesa, and Globe.

Arizona Game and Fish maintains a fish hatchery at the head of the stream and manages the 7.5-mile portion of the creek and tributaries within Tonto Forest as a "Blue-Ribbon" stream (artificials only, catch and release). Cattle were also fenced out from the stream bottom in the late 1980s, and the results have been remarkable: trout populations have increased four-fold. Floods have aggraded the banks, built up the plant community, and enhanced the fishery further, in contrast to other heavily grazed streams in the area, such as Cherry Creek, where floods decimate trout populations. Small side canyon **Mule Creek** holds wild trout in the headwaters, as do **Swamp Creek** and the lower end of **Willow Creek** (below **Rotten Spring**) farther below in the reservation.

To Show Low

Forestdale Cr

IR 48

Corduroy Cr

Hop Canyon Cr

US 60

AZ 73

To White River

The ideal conditions below the state fish hatchery persist for perhaps ten miles across the reservation boundary, whereupon Apache cattle find their way back along the streamcourse. The upland plant community here is ponderosa pine, Gambel oak, and Douglas fir. Stream temperatures are ideal for the many brown and rainbow trout that reside here in sizes averaging 8 inchs but ranging up to 20, with some even larger. On the reservation side, in particular, few of these fish ever see a fly. The elevation of the upper reservation stream is in the 5400-foot range—ice-cold water, warm sun, long growing season, good hatches from April through October, perfect conditions.

As Canyon Creek drops below 5000 feet over the next 10 miles, it starts to warm. The surrounding pine forests yield to juniper and then open oak savannas, and along the stream the alders and dogwoods yield ground to giant, shady sycamores, hackberry, velvet ash, and sumac. The white cobblestone on the bottom in the upper canyon, swept clean by the clear water, gives way to dark boulders, hidden in still, silt-bottomed pools seven to twenty feet deep. The water is green, the bottom brown and mossy. From the mouth of Bear Canyon down, only one rough road plus a few jeep tracks cross the canyon, and if you run into anyone else on the stream, count yourself lucky, or unlucky, as the case may be. In some sections weeks, months, can pass before

someone, either Apache or outsider, visits.

In this middle section of the creek around Bear Canyon, the trout are fewer in number but run larger. They tend to congregate in the deepest big pools below heavy water. In the 90 to 100 degree summer heat, the native suckers graze in the shallows and riffles in the full sunlight. Roundtail chubs feed in the runs and shaded, slow-moving pools, which are now a bit too warm for the browns and rainbows. Even an experienced fisherman will often mistake these fish for trout as they rise to take mayflies in the late afternoon and evening, all summer long. Clumsy-looking green sunfish, some as big as bluegills, are easily spotted in the sluggish eddies. These are very tasty when grilled on an juniper and driftwood campfire, they are exotic and unwanted in today's fisheries picture, and they are plentiful. Relax, have a few.

Farther downstream yet, the Oak Creek Ranch road branches off main tribal route 12 to cross Canyon Creek under the shade of giant cottonwoods at 4400 feet. A better campsite than this cannot be found. On a grassy knoll above the stream, the view is of the turrets, forested ridges, abrupt rims, and redrock canyons for which Arizona is famous the world over. From this camp it is 20 miles south and 1500 feet down to the Salt River. Trout are very scarce here, the catch being chubs, which you must release, smallmouth bass, which you may release if you wish, and green sunfish, which you are encouraged to eat. Yet if you do hook a trout in one of the big holes, look out. It could be the biggest one you've ever had on your line. Below the mouth of (dry) Oak Creek, the trout all but disappear, but a few hole up, how far down I don't know, and they have been caught in the Salt River below the creek.

CIBECUE CREEK

Name:	Cibecue Creek
Location:	Fort Apache Indian Reservation
Elevation:	6500-3900 feet
Average Volume:	8 cfs
Length of fishing water:	42 miles
Best Times:	April, May, September-November
Fish Species:	Brown trout, Arizona trout, Sonoran sucker, longfin dace,
Tributaries:	White Spring branch, CT Spring branch, Salt Creek

Cibecue Creek forms between two long, 7000-foot, north-south ridges, Chadeski and Carrizo. Its upper nine miles are usually dry but the lower 42 miles of the streamcourse have ample year-round flow, roughly 10 cfs on average in the lower reaches of the stream. The permanent water begins at **White Spring**. In its upper reaches, particularly the five-mile stretch between **CT Spring** and its namesake village, Cibecue is a superb spring creek, passing under the shade of a diverse, multi-story riparian *bosque* of Arizona walnut, narrowleaf cottonwoods, boxelders, alders, grape arbors, willows, watercresses, and many other streamside plant forms. The stream holds a stable, naturally reproducing population of brown trout. In the past it has produced some very large browns, up to 8 pounds. Located far from the reservation's tourist centers, for many years this stream seldom saw an angler of any kind, until the Apache tribe began to fish here in the 1950s and 1960s. During this time the hatchery truck visited several times a year providing rainbow trout. The rainbows are long gone, but in recent years the trucks have returned, now bearing Apache trout from Alchesay and Williams Creek hatcheries. These newcomers have spread through the stream, but one suspects that once the plantings stop, the Apache trout will go by the way, also.

White Spring is well named, its water a chalky blue-green capable of hiding surprisingly large numbers of fish. The spring arises in a picnic area accessible by dirt road (Tribal 34, eleven miles north of Cibecue Village) and only flows for a couple hundred yards before falling into the usually dry bed of Cibecue Creek. It is in this very brief stretch where most of the trout are to be found, for the smaller (.5-1 cfs) flow of the spring dissipates into the gravel once it reaches Cibecue's creekbed. Yet even in the dry of late spring and fall, scattered pools for the four to five stream miles do hide a few skittish fish.

At this point CT Spring roars out of the ground seven miles above the village of Cibecue, flowing through a jungle-like narrow but convenient rocky arroyo for a half-mile or so before entering Cibecue Creek proper. Brown and Apache trout live in the arroyo, all the way to the point where the spring gushes out of the ground. Many Apache folk don't like to fish here because of rattlesnakes, which do occur here, as they do elsewhere. The spring is constant, about 54 degrees, and larger than the creek itself, which could well be called CT Spring Creek after the arroyo enters. The wickiups and bean fields that used to dot Cibecue Creek bottom in the stream's middle reaches are dwindling away today, yielding to the willows and cottonwoods, and leaving the stream and old farmsites for the fly fisherman to appreciate and contemplate. Tributary **Salt Creek** enters here also with a few occasional trout near its mouth. Fishing under spring-creek conditions continues all the way to the Cibecue village. In the vicinity of the village, a sawmill looms on a platform above the creek, horses graze and trample along the banks, the bottom muddies, and irrigation ditches return their flow. June's late-afternoon water temperatures have now risen to close to 70 degrees by the time Cibecue Creek heads into its gorge six miles below the village, yet the browns persist in this stretch and even into the upper gorge. During the fall and winter months some of these fish are said (by locals) to drift even farther down where the warmwater minnows, suckers, and chubs start to take their proper place in the lower end of the stream. This lower end of Carrizo is a spectacular mini-Zion of falls and terraces.

At the very head of Cibecue Creek along the Mogollon Rim lie tiny **Wildhorse and Blue lakes,** both reachable by rough, hard-to-locate jeep roads from the north. Rainbows have been planted here from time to time. Check with the tribal game office in Whiteriver for directions and advice.

CARRIZO CREEK

Name:	Carrizo Creek
Location:	Fort Apache Indian Reservation,
Elevation:	7500-3700 feet
Length of Fishing Water:	53 miles
Best Times:	April, May, September-November
Fish Species:	Brown trout, rainbow trout, desert sucker, speckled dace, roundtail chub
Tributaries:	Corduroy Creek, Forestdale Creek, Hop Canyon, Limestone Canyon

Carrizo Creek is scattered all over the low-lying central portion of the White Mountain Apache Reservation. Its watershed is quite large, but water collects sporadically, the quality of the water varies, and to fish this system you need to find its isolated pockets of permanent water. When you do find these places, the fishing can be very good or very poor, typical of most degraded watersheds in the Southwest still holding trout populations.

The upper reaches of the Carrizo are a broad sweep of ponderosa pine. The drainage sweeps to the southeast, with many small shaded canyons fanning out on the north side and spreading under the rim, all dry. There is not a really major cold spring in the whole upper watershed. About half of the major side canyons have rough roads leading up to the rim and the rest are roadless. If there are any undiscovered pockets of trout habitat remaining in Arizona, this area would be the most likely place to find one. The canyon bottom of Carrizo Creek itself is more open, forming a broad valley in places, and it is loaded with cattle. Good, reliable water begins at 5200 feet below the mouth of Mud Creek, about 10 miles above the Carrizo Village, and it is in this stretch where the stream's occasional trout may be found, along with native species like Sonoran sucker and roundtail chubs. Tributary **Limestone Canyon**, another marginal coldwater fishery, enters about four miles above the village. This is a beautiful place to camp in and explore in the fall, though it's quite hot in June. If you find a few wild trout, count it as a bonus. If not, enjoy the *alter* trout, the chubs, which you can catch with Elk Hair Caddis, Adams, or Hare's Ear Nymphs.

It is at Carrizo village that Carrizo Creek meets its major tributary. **Corduroy Creek** forms beneath Pinetop, Amos and Cooley mountains, all about 7400 feet high, just across AZ Highway 73 from the busy, brand-new Hondah gambling casino. Two headwater ponds provide some trout fishing. **Cooley Tank**, an old 5-acre stock pond at 7050 feet, was named after a scout for General Crook who was able to "Show Low," thus winning an important poker game and naming the nearby town of Showlow, Arizona. The newer, 6800-foot **Bootleg Lake**, like Cooley Tank, yields an interesting combination of sunfish, channel catfish, catch-and-release Florida strain largemouth bass, and brown trout. Below these impoundments, Corduroy Creek flows westward from 7000 to 6000 feet through various cattle ranches, roughly parallel to the rim, dropping underground here and there, then re-appearing below scattered permanent springs. These springs keep the water cool, and occasional beaver ponds provide enough depth for fish to survive. The water is almost always muddy, due to a poor watershed and many cattle, but there are also a few trout. Tributary **Forestdale Creek** entering at 6000 feet has a much larger reliable flow from big (warm) springs just above its confluence with Corduroy, and is even muddier. There are a very few trout in the upper reaches of this stream, generally above the beaver dams, and scads of roundtail chubs below the springs.

Below Forestdale mouth, Corduroy is strictly a warmwater stream, flowing down a scenic canyon parallel to US 60, the main route from Phoenix to the White Mountains, before joining and warming Carrizo Creek, whereupon the canyon continues to its mouth into the Salt River at 4100 feet. One small side stream, **Hop Canyon**, has a good spring at 5600 feet and may hold trout, also, though I haven't tried it.

10. WHITE RIVER SYSTEM

Name: White River
Location: Fort Apache Indian Reservation
Maps: USGS 1:100,000 series, Nutrioso edition
Elevation: 10,000 feet at extreme headwater tributaries to 4800 feet at the Salt River
Average Volume: 150 cfs
Length of Fishing Water: 85 miles (including North Fork)
Best Times: April, May, September-November
Fish Species: Apache and brown trout, rainbow trout, Sonoran sucker, longfin dace
Fishable Tributaries: Many, see below. An asterisk (*) denotes waters closed to the public
North Fork White River: Diamond Creek, Coon Creek (Diamond Creek), Little Diamond Creek (Diamond Creek), Cienega Creek (Little Diamond Creek), unnamed tributary. (Little Diamond Creek), Coyote Creek*, Maverick Cienega outlet*, unnamed tributary (Little Diamond Creek)*, Sun Creek*, tributary*, Moon Creek*, tributary*, Star Creek*, North Fork Diamond Creek*, headwater branch*, Bull Cienega Creek, Gooseberry Creek, Gomez Creek, Trout Creek, Earl Creek*, Porcupine Creek, Williams Creek, Sand Creek, Lame Deer Canyon, Bog Creek, Little Bog Creek, Soldier Creek, Horseshoe Creek, Bar H Creek, No Name Creek, Paradise Creek, Snow Stake Creek, Wohlenberg Draw, Bear Cienega and Creek, Sheep Cienega, Ord Creek*, Smith Creek*, Snake Creek, Becker Creek, Sunrise Creek
East Fork White River: Firebox Creek, Rock Creek (plus 3 unnamed tributaries), Deep Creek (plus one unnamed tributary)*, Elk Canyon (plus one unnamed tributary.)*, three upper unnamed tributaries*.

The centerpiece of the lofty White Mountains, 11,400-foot Mount Baldy and its neighboring sister peaks are the eroded rim of an ancient volcanic field. The spruce-covered Baldy is not really bald—timberline this far south is closer to 12,000 feet—but is still high enough to pull summer rain from the Gulf of Mexico and winter snow from the Gulf of California, giving rise to Arizona's largest permanent river, the **Salt**, whose headwaters form an almost complete circle around the mountain. Ditched for irrigation by the Maricopa Indians thousands of years ago, the river was dammed in its lower reaches between the Mazatzal and Superstition ranges at the turn of the century to provide for downstream cotton fields in Maricopa County. The Salt is essentially a desert stream. Below the dams in the chain of reservoirs at the river's lower end provided by the ninety-year-old Salt River Project,

the Salt provides some tailwater fishing for rainbow trout spilled over from the lakes, and winter fishing for planted rainbows almost all the way down to the suburbs of Phoenix.

In its roadless fifty miles of steep upper canyon, the Salt is an entirely different creature, a free-flowing wilderness river, where it is formed at the base of the White Mountain high country by the join of the Black and the White rivers. The Black forms on the southeast flank of the Baldy, the White on the west and north. Together these two smallish rivers provide for nearly half of Arizona's current trout habitat, with over 100 tributary trout streams in the upper reaches of the mountains; most of them flow 7000 feet or more above sea level through Canada-like coniferous forests covered by deep snow in the winter months. The trout season here also corresponds to that of Michigan's Upper Peninsula, Canada, or Montana. Many mountain roads aren't clear of snow until late April or early May.

Of the two systems, the White River drains the Fort Apache Indian Reservation, while the slightly smaller Black arises and flows principally through the Apache National Forest. Public fishing within the White River watershed is allowed by the White Mountain Apache tribe on about half the streams of the reservation, and daily licenses are available through the tribal-owned White Mountain Recreation Enterprises. Closures, fees, and special waters may vary yearly. The information included here is approximate and up-to-date only as of the time of publication. A word to the wise: Although the closed waters of the Apache tribal lands can be as tempting as the roadside streams of Yellowstone Park, the tribe does not coddle game offenders. Expect a heavy fine plus quite possible confiscation of your equipment and vehicle should you ignore tribal regulations.

The **White River** mainstem flows below the mountain, in low-elevation summer heat. It is a short stream, providing better habitat for smallmouth bass than for trout. Twenty miles above its mouth, it is formed just below the town of Whiteriver, AZ at 5000 feet, by the confluence of its North and East Forks as they tumble straight down from the mountains, and it is in the two forks that the real trout fishing in White River system actually begins, extending upstream almost to the very tops of the mountains.

The upper White River watershed, snowed in from November till April, is managed mainly for the native Arizona trout, *O. apache*, with an eventual goal of reclaiming as many waters as possible for this fascinating species. The trout was formally named after the Apaches in 1974, to note the lead the tribe had taken in protecting the rare trout. Many of the Apache stocks have already been affected by earlier rainbow plantings, and the type most commonly caught in some of the more accessible tributaries is a rainbow *x* Arizona hybrid. One tell-tale sign of a pure-strain Apache or Arizona trout is the black mask formed by prominent black spots on the body just outside the eye. Many of the Apache-type trout found in the reservation now lack this mask. Rainbows are no longer planted in reservation streams and for a time the tribe also refrained from planting them in the impounded lakes scattered throughout the higher elevations of the eastern portion of the reservation. The native Apache trout planted in the lakes in place of the rainbows, however, were found to be difficult to catch by the conventional Wal-Mart baitfishing methods employed by most Phoenicians and other city-bound tourists. These people do most of the camping, so to provide more angler success and tourist satisfaction the tribe recently resumed limited rainbow stocking in a number of the lakes.

The significant wild-trout fishery on the Apache reservation consists of both Apache trout and brook char at the highest waters, generally above 9000 feet, Apache trout and browns trout in the lower headwaters, and browns in the bigger streams from 5000 feet up, although some browns can be found in scattered sites at lower elevations. Brown trout in particular dominate the fishing picture in the White Mountains, both on and off the reservation. Although Apache trout from the Williams and Alchesay federal hatcheries are now pumped into a few selected reservation waters by the hundreds of thousands each year, they have little effect on wild trout populations, and wild Apache trout stocks remain vulnerable to encroachment and displacement from brookies above in some waters and by browns below in nearly all waters. The browns, in particular, have been gradually ascending from the larger streams into the small tributary refuges for the native trout. The tribe has tried to protect pure populations with stone-and-chicken-wire barriers placed across streams selected to be either protected or reclaimed, but change so far has been slow to come and in many waters the browns continue to encroach upstream. The remaining pure-strain Apache trout streams lie mainly on the highest mountain lands, those surrounding Mount Baldy, most of which have been closed to entry by the White Mountain Apache tribe.

NORTH FORK OF THE WHITE RIVER

The **North Fork** of the White is a big stream, up to 50 feet wide in its lower reaches, and a favored swimming hole for Apache children in the village of Whiteriver. North of town, teenagers like to camp, party, and swim in the canyon below the Alchesay hatchery. Browns are there if you can find a quiet spot, say, during school hours. Hatchery Apache trout are also stocked regularly. For three or four miles above Alchesay the canyon is less accessible and the stream offers a lot of overlooked fishing for browns, including some really nice fish of 20 or more inches, and more hatchery natives (this term an *oxymoron*) above the old Roberts Ranch site. The river contains a fairly heavy sediment load and muddies quickly after rains, a result of extensive recent heavy logging in the middle reaches of the watershed. Use of the North Fork becomes heavy again in the upstream campground country, first at Lower Log campground near the mouth of Bluff Cienega, then from Trout Creek mouth all the way up to Ditch Camp at 7600 feet. Campgrounds are right along the stream, with turnoffs marked by paper plates nailed to trees. The camping areas go on for miles. Old turn-offs and roads form a maze leading to the river—some of these tourists are allowed to use, most they are not. A walk of a mile or so will you get past the spur roads and between campgrounds. Go more than half a mile from these roads and you are by yourself, where the browns are generally small but quite catchable.

Above the ditch leadouts used to form small **A-1 Lake** (24 acres, 8800 feet) and other impoundments, the river branches into its roadless headwaters, each containing wild, pure-strain

Apaches mixed in with browns below and brook char above. The top of the White Mountains contains former refuges of pure-strain Apache trout, such as pristine, meadow-rimmed **Ord Creek***, nine miles long and flowing from 10,000 to 9000 feet right under its 11,350-foot namesake mountain. Most of the extreme headwaters of the North Fork have been invaded by the brookies. These char reproduce far faster than the natives, reaching sexual maturity at 2 to 3 years of age. Some tiny tributaries are crammed with three-inch fish. They don't seem to know when to stop breeding. Both **Ord** and its tributary twin, 3-mile-long **Smith Creek***, are currently protected from logging, but not from the brook char.

Becker Creek, 3.5 miles of excellent water, originates in two branches on the ski slopes of Sunrise Mountain and joins with 1-mile-long **Snake Creek** to form the North Fork itself just below Sunrise Lake. This used to be one of the main White Mountain fishing destinations, where heroic anglers could catch Apache trout by the hundreds. One turn-of-the-century photo shows a stringer of some 500 fish, the result of an afternoon's sport. Today you'll find only browns, plus a few brookies up at the top of the stream. Brookies are a favorite species in high-elevation reservoirs like **Sunrise Lake**, a flooded 9130-foot meadow near the junction of Snake Creek with **Sunrise Creek.** This shallow depression, enhanced by a low dam, is filled by snowmelt each spring and at 875 acres represents the largest coldwater reservoir in the state. The state record brook char (4 pounds, 15 ounces) was landed here in October of 1995. Apache trout, rainbows, and grayling are also planted.

Just to the north between Mount Baldy and 10,500-foot Greens Peak is a high-elevation meadow where tiny, 9000-foot **Horseshoe Creek** arises as the first northern tributary to the North Fork. This slow-moving little meadow rill holds trout, disappears in *cienegas* and bogs during spring melt and all but dries out in the late summer and fall. The level upper meadow is criss-crossed with tribal roads, and not surprisingly the native Apache trout have all but disappeared here. Farther west and a few hundred feet lower in elevation, the creek enters 1000-acre **Horseshoe Cienega**, where it is joined by a 3.5-mile-long meadowy brown trout stream, **Bar H Creek.** Cattle congregate in the old *cienega*, now merely a grassy pasture, affecting the fishing. The juncture of the two streams is in a small enclosure holding marsh plants and a few fish. This is just above sedge-filled, shallow, murky **Horseshoe Cienega Lake.** The 120-acre lake, on the lower edge of the cienega at 8200 feet, complete with store and boat rentals, is sometimes enhanced by a flume leading down from the North Fork. Many well-fed browns are here, plus a few Apache and rainbow trout. In fact, Horseshoe Cienega Lake has yielded the Arizona record brown trout—16 pounds, 7 ounces. Below the dam, Horseshoe Creek continues on to the North Fork a mile below where small browns and an occasional Apache trout survive in tiny beaver ponds and a minicanyon, which sometimes dries out completely. On the other side of the North Fork a few miles above here, tiny **Bear Cienega Creek***, 3.5 miles long and holding wild browns, gives a more

. . .Continued on page 41

Dragonfly nymph

Arizona FISHING WATERS

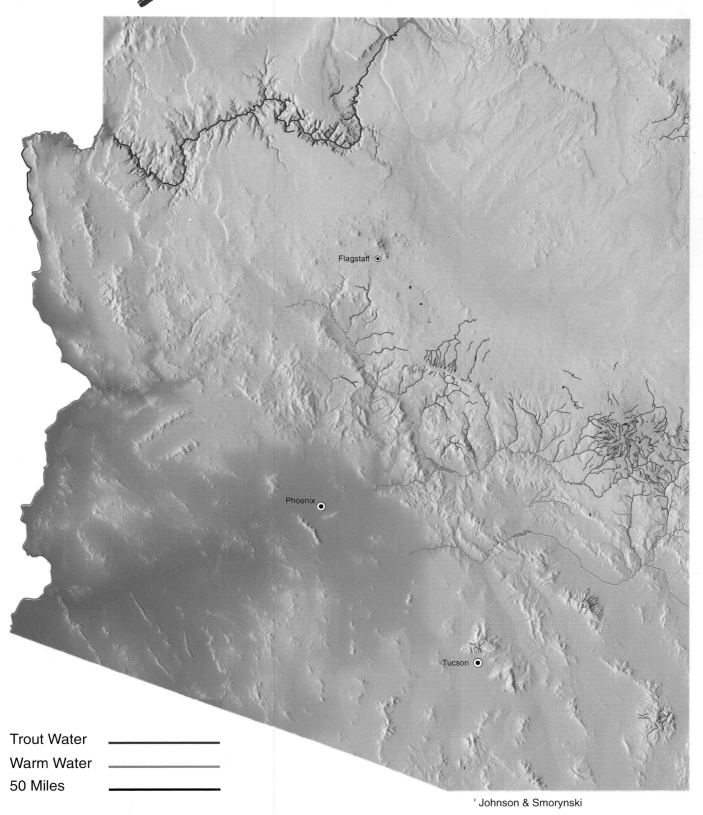

Flagstaff ◉

Phoenix ◉

Tucson ◉

Trout Water ————————

Warm Water ————————

50 Miles ————————

' Johnson & Smorynski

The author fishing near the Arizona New Mexico state line.

Oak Creek, north of Sedona Coconino National Forest.

Workman Creek above confluence with Salome Creek; Hells Hole area of the Salome Wilderness, Tonto National Forest, north of Globe.

The famous Oak Creek Canyon just north of Sedona. Coconino National Forest.

Blue River just west of the New Mexico state line. Apache-Sitgreaves National Forest.

Spider Rock in Canyon De Chelly, Navajo Indian Reservation. Although there are no trout in the canyon, some may be found close to the stream's source in the Chuska Mountains just to the east about 15 miles. (Tribal permits required for camping)

Chitty Falls just south of Mogollon Rim on the East Fork of Eagle Creek. Apache-Sitgreaves National Forest.

View from south rim of the Grand Canyon near Shoshone Point.

Cathedral Rock above Cave Creek in the Chiricahua Mountains near the village of Portal. Part of the the Coronado National Forest.

Chevelon Creek, north of the Mogollon Rim, Apache-Sitgreaves National Forest.

Suspension bridge crossing Colorado River near Phantom Ranch in the Grand Canyon.

CT spring just above Cibecue Creek on the Fort Apache Indian Reservation. (Fishing and camping permits required.)

Blue River Box. JAY SCOTT PHOTO.

POPULAR PATTERNS FOR *Arizona* WATERS

Trico Spinner

Light Cahill

Parachute Adams

Parachute
Blue-winged Olive

Elk Hair Caddis

Stimulator

Madam "X"

Joe's Hopper

Parachute Hopper

Noruis' Hopper

Out of the Blue Emerger

Stonefly

Prince Nymph

Reservoir Fly

Peacock Lady

reliable flow. This steep stream forms just north of Mt. Ord at 10,000 feet. An old road grade parallels the stream for its entire length, but the entire length is at present closed to the public.

Next to enter the North Fork from the south is a very fine stream aptly named **Paradise Creek.** Its 12 miles of prime trout habitat hold pure-strain Apache trout in its upper 4 to 8 miles, reaching steeply up to the foot of 11,000-foot Mt. Warren, while browns mix with the Apaches in the beaver-filled lower portions. Only the lower 2 miles of the stream are open to the public. This section is reachable via tribal road Y24 which parallels the upper North Fork from Hawley Lake junction, crossing Paradise Creek 7 miles or so from the junction. Upper tributaries **Wohlenberg Draw*** and one-mile **Snow Stake Creek*** hold browns and Apaches, but are both closed.

Two small brown trout streams, **Bog Creek and Soldier Creek** form in meadows under 9300-foot Soldier Butte near the northern boundary of the reservation, then join together at **Bog Tank** (18 acres, 8200 feet, browns and rainbows) on the edge of Horseshoe Cienega (see above). Bog Creek continues westward from here just north of AZ 260 acquiring 3-mile brown trout mini-tributary **Little Bog Creek**, while forming first **Big Bear (Shush Be Tou),** then downstream **Little Bear (Shush Be Zahze) Lake** at 7800 and 7900 feet, respectively. Both lakes are of the put-and-take, campground variety, with hatchery rainbows and Apaches provided twice a month in summer. Wild browns are also here, and green sunfish in the upper lake. Below the Bear lakes, Bog Creek narrows up and provides a home for wild rainbows and browns of 6 to 10 inches in slow-moving current that becomes a sequence of still pools by late summer. Crossing AZ 260 before falling steeply into the North Fork's Canyon, the stream is alive with crayfish which grow almost as large as the fish. A few jumbo-sized browns inhabit the occasional deep holes. The flow I have seen here is 1 to 2 cfs on the average. Access is by foot. Immediately below Bog Creek a tiny, **unnamed feeder** holding a very few browns enters the North Fork.

On the other, south side of the river, first 3-mile **No-Name Creek** then 5-mile **Sand Creek** enter. The tiny No-Name, at times almost a tunnel through alders, grapevines, willows, and narrowleaf cottonwoods, holds Apache trout in its narrow canyon. Sand Creek is somewhat larger but equally overgrown in its lower end. Browns have invaded this stream. **Cyclone Lake,** at 40 acres, is formed at 8150 feet by Sand Creek and tributary **Lame Deer Canyon*.** This lake is available by reservation only—the whole lake, that is, at $300 a day plus $3 per person. It holds rainbow and Apache trout, plus browns, some 10 pounds or more.

As the North Fork of the White River moves downstream its canyon becomes so deep and pronounced that an entire stream, **Williams Creek**, is formed below the canyon rim from a rushing spring at 6600 feet. Here is the Williams Creek National Fish Hatchery, whose job it is to produce hundreds of thousands of Apache trout clones each season. Oddly enough, the clones do not survive very well in the natal waters of *O. apache*. Most die within a few weeks. Few if any reproduce. Just below the hatchery is an Apache youth camp, which has a couple of large beaver ponds fenced off from the cattle and producing lush growth of cattails and bullrushes. These ponds and the gorgeous 1 or 2 miles of stream below provide a constant food supply for wild rainbows

only—the Apache clones seem unable to get a toehold in their own hatchery stream, the rainbows separated from the hatchery only by a modest barbed wire fence.

Just below Williams Creek, the North Fork canyon turns abruptly to the south, heading directly for Whiteriver, Arizona and confluence with the East Fork. As it turns, it acquires the flow of **Gooseberry Creek** from the north and **Trout Creek** from the south. Gooseberry flows east to west a long way, 14 miles or so, but doesn't hold much water during dry periods. Years ago there were campgrounds upstream reachable via dirt road from the old reservation lumber town of McNary, and rainbows were stocked, but now the rough roads north of AZ 260 are closed and the trout (mostly rainbows and rainbow-Apache hybrids) are smaller, but wild. The best fishing is within the gorge of the North Fork on the lower 2 miles of the stream. Here 3-mile tributary **Gomez Creek** enters. I've caught the little Apaches up to 16 inches from this stream, which gets much of its water from the bullhead and pike-filled mill ponds in McNary, once used to float giant ponderosa sawlogs.

Sandy-bottomed **Trout Creek**, 7 miles long and entering from the south, contains browns (some of which show swollen heads and other signs of possible hatchery-based infection) and is notable mainly for its upper reservoir, 260-acre **Hawley Lake.** The lake, reachable by paved road from AZ 260 at 8200 feet, receives many stockings through the summer and holds brook, rainbow, brown, and even stocked Apache trout. Hawley's east shore contains a number of former summer homes no longer in use, except by the cattle grazing on the old lawns, and meadow tributary **Earl Creek*** passes by a number of these on its way from 8250-foot, 38-acre **Earl Park Lake** a half mile away. The lake is catch and release, artificial lures only, and yields the same species as Hawley. The creek ranges 3 miles upstream from the lake. Both it and its 1-mile tributary **Porcupine Creek*,** plus yet another **unnamed tributary*,** hold many beaver and large browns; all are closed to fishing.

As the North Fork heads south for Whiteriver, it parallels AZ 78, the road to Pinetop, Whiteriver, and the new casino at the former roadside stop of Hondah ("welcome," in Apache). The river's gorge is visible from this road, but not the water, shaded by 50- to 80-ft cottonwood trees. The highway also passes directly over 5.4-mile **Bull Cienega Creek**, which holds browns and Apache trout. In the lower reaches of the stream are small waterfalls. Out of earshot from these, you can pull trout from quiet pools while listening to the occasional whizzing of cars overhead.

DIAMOND CREEK SYSTEM

Just before entering Whiteriver, the North Fork gains the flow of its major tributary, **Diamond Creek.** This is a smaller version of the North Fork, fifteen miles long, silty below, clearer upstream, with its own generous share of campgrounds in the lower end. It forms on the north slope of 10,800-foot Diamond Butte, just to the west of the Mt. Baldy complex of peaks. The fishing on the creek's lower end is slow under the giant cottonwood trees for a few very nice browns (to 20 inches or more), except when the Williams Creek stockers are deposited for easy removal by tourists and tribal members alike. The current is 20 feet wide or more, and provides ample room in the cottonwood shade for 50-foot fly-casts and an upstream approach to the good pools interspersed regularly with rapids and shallow riffles. Stinging nettle, always a sign of good trout habitat in the White Mountains, abounds in summer months on the banks of this creek near the North Fork confluence, oil-change and beer party litter abounds year round.

These lower-end conditions are in contrast with superb wild brown water in the middle reaches and the still wild country and generous supply of small tributaries in the upper stream, each with Arizona trout populations. The uncrowded middle and upper reaches of Diamond Creek provide wild browns of 8 to 10 inches, with some wary specimens ranging to 16 inches or more. Sunset and evening fishing with small nymphs almost always yields browns in the summer months, especially after the typical late-afternoon rains. **Coon Creek** has 2.5 miles of water in a narrow canyon below Horse Mesa. A few native, pure-strain Apache trout may persist here, with bigger ones near the head of the stream. Farther upstream, **North Fork Diamond Creek*** has a hundred-acre beaver dam and wet meadow complex at its confluence with the main branch of Diamond. It is 3 miles long and holds browns, plus Apache trout of unknown purity. Half-mile-long **Star Creek*** is also part of this large marsh, containing its share of the same trout. Farther up near the head of Diamond Creek is an **unnamed tributary*** falling off Diamond Butte and possibly holding a remnant population of Apache trout.

A bit farther up, 40-acre **Christmas Tree Lake** at 8200 feet was formed in 1965 at the join of **Sun and Moon creeks*,** just a half-mile upstream from Diamond Creek, to provide brood stock for what was essentially a wild-to-wild stocking program for the Apache trout. The original stock was acquired from Ord Creek, which has since been invaded by brook char. The lake, named for a White House Christmas tree cut nearby in 1962, is managed under special regulations and provides enough water to grow 15- to 18 inch Apache trout, with some quite a bit larger. The Apaches spawn in the two creeks, as well as in two **sub-tributaries*** farther up. The world-record Apache trout, 5 pounds 12 ounces, was landed here in 1995. These are wild, reproducing fish, the progeny of a single planting in 1970. They readily take dry flies and follow late-morning, mid-day, and evening hatches, mid-June to early September. Browns have somehow also managed to gain entry to this Apache trout preserve, growing up to 8 pounds. You are allowed to keep nine of these but only one Apache trout of 16-inch minimum size. It takes a special permit to fish here, costing anywhere from 6 to 25 dollars per day, depending on the time of year. The two meadow-rimmed creeks above the lake, each about 5 miles long and closed to the public, hold wild Apaches and browns of considerably smaller size.

Little Diamond Creek, joining with main Diamond at 6500 feet near the Y 26 road and heading at 9400 feet beneath a long ridge just west of Mount Ord, is 13 miles long, with the upper 8 miles closed by the tribe. Excellent fishing for browns of up to 16 inches is what you always find here and in several tributaries, also, at least during years of good rainfall. The stream is uniformly brushy and hard to approach. During the rainy season, the browns become active every evening, and you can fish with dries with good success—provided you can find casting room. The water is clear enough to bring fish off the bottom with an Adams or Blue-winged Olive, and in the beaver pond areas this is the way to go. More often, however, it is easier to dap nymphs and let them sink

and drift under alder branches or along undercut banks. The tributaries are even harder to fish. Extremely small **Cienega Creek**, about a mile long, enters Little Diamond from the north at 7400 feet. You'll probably miss it where it crosses tribal land south of Hawley Lake. Hidden by grasses here, it holds small Apache trout plus a few browns. **Coyote Creek*,** small and closed to the public, flows for three miles and held pure-strain Apache trout as late as the 1980s, but these have been all but driven out by the browns, some of very respectable size. Coyote Creek joins Little Diamond among extensive beaver ponds right at the tribal road R26 crossing 4 miles south of Hawley Lake. The stream and tributaries are closed above this crossing, open below. **Maverick Cienega and Creek,** similar in size and nature to Coyote, have two miles of water and enter just below the pond area. Open to fishing, the stream may still hold wild Apaches. Above the road crossing, a pair of **unnamed tributaries*** enter Little Diamond at about 8400 feet. These hold browns, too, but are closed and virtually never fished.

EAST FORK SYSTEM

The **East Fork** of the White River, 31 miles long and a bit smaller than the North Fork, is steep and cold, containing wild, pure-strain Apache trout in its closed, roadless upper reaches and wild browns plus stocked Apache trout in the public water below. The lower six miles pass along broad cottonwood groves through an open valley overlooked by the looming Nine Mile Ridge. Here the stream is paralleled by a paved road lined with small farms. The water warms and turns brown as it prepares to meet the North Fork under broad palisades of White Mountain basalt. This lower end is silt-bottomed, the silt swept away below occasional rapids, and provides fair fishing for mostly small browns, with a very occasional giant.

Farther upstream above the tribal road crossing at Rock Creek mouth, the East Fork becomes extremely steep; the browns become more numerous but not much larger. At the uppermost six miles of the stream wild Apaches replace the browns at last.

The East Fork has a few tributaries, all providing significant Apache trout habitat but not too much in the way of fishing, simply because most are closed to the public. **Elk Canyon*,** one of the best, has 8 miles of prime Apache trout water, all closed. During this course it plunges from nearly 9000 to 7400 feet, with one equally steep, trout-bearing **mini-tributary*.** Larger, lower-elevation **Rock Creek,** lined with willows, is easily accessible by tribal 55 twelve miles east of Whiteriver, holding 9 miles of Apache trout habitat (some fish at the lower end are of unknown purity), plus at least three unnamed tributaries also holding the rare native trout. These and other headwater tributaries become nearly dry during October and June, but the trout seek standing pools of water and survive there. **Deep Creek*** flows under 10,000-foot Aspen Ridge, is 10 miles long with a 1-mile **unnamed tributary*** and is full of pure-strain Apache trout; it's also closed to the public. Similar in nature to Rock Creek, willow-choked **Firebox Creek** is a low-elevation stream holding about 8 miles of trout habitat. Intermittent in its lower end, it flows towards but not always into the lower East Fork: the creek is generally dry for its last couple of miles. In dry weather many other reaches will turn into discrete pools of water, but these will all hold pure-strain Apache trout. Though you can't see it, the flow of the creek remains, passing beneath the stones and gravel of the bed, still fresh and cold.

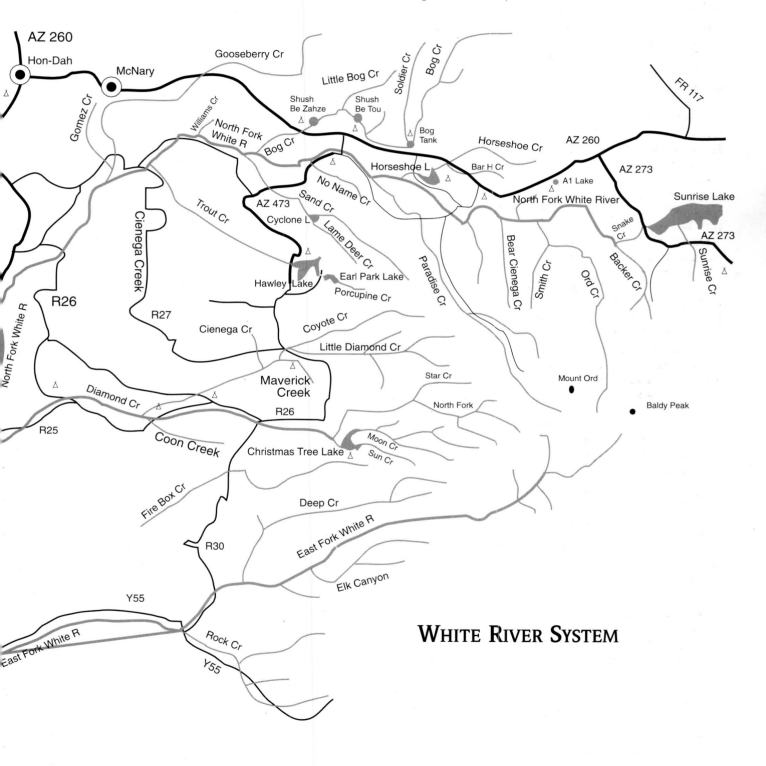

WHITE RIVER SYSTEM

11. BONITO CREEK SYSTEM

Name: Bonito Creek
Location: Fort Apache Indian Reservation
Maps: USGS 1:100,000 series, Nutrioso edition
Elevation: 7000-3900 feet
Length of Fishing Water: 42 miles
Best Times: June-October, September-November
Fish Species: Brown trout, rainbow trout, Apache trout, smallmouth bass, Sonoran sucker, longfin dace
Fishable Tributaries: Peasoup, Duke, and Hughey Creeks, Hurricane Creek, Flash Creek, Long Canyon, 4 unnamed tributaries, Lofer Cienega, Butterfly Cienega, Squaw Creek, Little Bonito Creek, Bog Creek, Crooked Creek, Tonto Creek, Bull Creek, Cienega Creek

Arising on the southern flank of 11450-foot Mount Baldy and flowing southwestward for 40 miles before falling into the Black River canyon, hard-to-reach **Bonito Creek** is arguably the best stream in Arizona. It is good trout water from top to bottom. Some sections of this river-sized, high-elevation stream and its tributaries are so remote they don't see anglers for months or even years. Water quality is superb, and many upper tributaries are among the last strongholds for wild, original-strain Apache trout. These headwaters flow through dense, sometimes claustrophobic sub-alpine and mixed conifer forests and are overgrown with high-elevation mountain-lover dogwood and willow thickets, blue spruce, and bracken fern. This is more like British Columbia than the Southwest. Some of the Apache trout populations in this Canadian Shangri-la stem from original, well-adapted stream populations, not wild-to-wild relocations or hatchery re-plants. Bonito is very steep in its upper reaches, dropping 3000 feet in its first 9 miles—much steeper than the other major streams radiating from Mount Baldy, with their lower-gradient-headwater meadows.

In its lower end Bonito cuts a sharply incised course through beautiful, high-elevation Bonito Prairie, its green gallery forests of cottonwoods and willows, boxelders, and walnut passing several hundred feet beneath the gramma grasses and Indian paintbrush of the prairie above. I once lost a monster brown in lower Bonito, well over two feet long, so large that my daughter was later afraid to wade across the lower end of the rather smallish pool that held it. It seems that all the trout are large here; they *average* 15 to 16 inches, many reaching 20 to 25 (the biggest for me about three pounds); the brown-colored smallmouth bass which crowd into the still pools also run large for such a small river, averaging twelve inches or more. At 5280 feet, Bonito passes into the Black River canyon in the wilderness at the base of the pine-covered, 7900-foot Natanes Mountains of the San Carlos Apache Reservation. These lands are used by some cattle, somewhat more elk, deer, and bear, but are hardly touched by fishermen.

The major access for the upper stream is via the Reservation Lake-Whiteriver Road (tribal Y55), rough but graded and open only in summer. The upstream portion, about 6 miles worth, is within the tribe-only area where no fishing is allowed. The upper

9 miles of Bonito Creek are slated to be reclaimed for pure-strain Apache trout by 1999. Way up at 9000 feet, just below where Bonito is formed, 2-mile sub-tributary **Peasoup Creek*** trickles together with the larger streamlet. Native Apaches and possibly some brown trout invaders inhabit this collection of miniature plunge pools and waterfalls. Four miles below, **Duke Creek***, only a half mile long but with reliable water, adds its share of trout at 8200 feet. **Hughey Creek***, 4 to 5 miles long, is next to enter at 8100 feet, just above Hurricane Creek, and holds the same mixture of browns and natives. This stream is steep, narrow, and also small. The much larger **Hurricane Creek*** is dammed near its source at 8940 feet to form meadow-rimmed, 20-acre **Hurricane Lake.** "Renovated" in the late 1980s to remove all remaining browns, both the lake and the 2 miles of creek above the small dam now hold pure-strain Apache trout up to 20 inches in length. To catch these will cost you—the lake, accessible by rough road turnoff from tribal Y20, lies in the closed area surrounding Mount Baldy. The charge is $300 a day plus $5 per person, in advance, for exclusive use of the lake for your party. Only artificial lures are allowed, and only one trout of minimum 16 inches may be kept. If you stray below the dam, the lower 5 miles of the creek still hold browns, plus Apache trout of undetermined purity.

Tribal road Y55 crosses Bonito at 7900 feet, just above the mouth of tiny, micro-habitat **Butterfly Creek**, and it is only below this crossing that the stream and its tributaries become public water. Passing Bonito's whitewater chutes filled with Apache and brown trout, the road soon crosses brushy, tumbling **Squaw and Flash creeks,** ten and eleven miles long, respectively. These twin creeks empty into the bigger stream just above and below the mouth of **Long Canyon Creek** and another **unnamed tributary** (each of these tiny streams holding browns). The upper seven miles of Flash and Squaw creeks are closed to the public. Browns had almost entirely taken over these former Apache trout strongholds by 1990 (Flash had a remnant population as recently as 1983), but a few Apaches still survived here and there. All are currently being reclaimed for the native trout, with success still pending.

LITTLE BONITO

The Little Bonito system is roughly a mirror image of the Big Bonito. Little Bonito and its several tributaries hold many miles of fine Apache and brown trout water. The two systems join at about 6100 feet in some of the most remote country in the White Mountains. **Little Bonito Creek** itself is only 15 miles long and very steep, but it acquires a lot more water than its length would indicate. By Arizona standards it is a major stream. The trout arrangement here is also identical to Big Bonito, the upper reaches of the stream and tributaries are closed to the public, hold Apache trout, plus invading browns, and are slated for full recovery. The lower reaches are open for fishing and have been taken over by the browns, with rainbow trout of 12 to 14 inches also showing up on occasion. **Lofer Creek,** passing through a large namesake cienega, offers 7 miles of pure-strain Apache trout habitat. The upper 4 miles of water are closed. Sub-tributary **Boggy Creek**, 6 miles long, holds pure-strain Apache trout and empties into Lofer Creek about half a mile below tribal road Y55. This short reach is the only portion of this stream open to the public.

Crooked Creek is about 6 miles in length and holds browns in its lower reaches, Apaches in its upper part. The whole of the Little Bonito system, including two **unnamed tributaries**, is slated for "renovation," that is to say, the removal of browns and re-introduction of Apaches in the lower portions. The 3 miles above the Y55 road are closed.

After acquiring water from the Little Bonito, Bonito Creek moves into lower elevations and becomes a miniature version of the lower Black River, passing through low-lying benches filled with grassy groves of ponderosa pine. This reach continues all the way to the mouth of Tonto Creek (see below) where the Bonito leaves the forest and enters Bonito Prairie. Big pools in this reach hold trophy brown trout, plus a few rainbows that run nearly as large. The most reliable access is on foot, following the stream bottom which has by now leveled out for easier hiking—not an ideal grade, but do-able. This is a trout fisherman's dream. A week's hiking trip in August or September leaves you alone on the stream with pine breezes and brilliant sunshine. Standard equipment should include good wading sandals, nylon shorts, and plenty of sunscreen.

TONTO CREEK

Final Bonito tributary **Tonto Creek** joins the larger stream at 5700 feet just above the Bonito Prairie. This is another excellent tribal trout habitat, 24 miles long and flowing for most of its length in a well-defined canyon beneath extensive ponderosa pine tablelands and ridges. A much smaller stream than Bonito, Tonto Creek is even cleaner and colder where the two join. Errant cattle have cleaned out a good share of the willows and sedges on lower Bonito, clearing grasses from the benches and leaving in their wake thickets of poison ivy, but fewer invade the narrow confines of Tonto Creek. Though in some stretches the stream can get brushy and enclosed by the willow thickets, evening fishing for browns is superb here, June through September. Arizona has two Tonto Creeks, both excellent trout streams.

Near its head at 7000 feet, Tonto Creek is dammed to form 82-acre **Tonto Lake*** (closed to the public). The stream doesn't form on the Mount Baldy snowfields, but rather on the south flank of pine-crested, 8500-foot Odart Mountain. There are few tributaries here, because of the lower, drier elevation, but what few there are, are worth finding. Browns thrive in clean, cold sub-tributaries **Cienega Creek** and **Bull Creek**, each about 2 miles in length, draining 8100-foot Maverick Mountain and entering Tonto from the south. Just to the south, the Natanes Mountains are only a few hundred feet lower and filled with pine forests, yet contain no real trout streams and very little permanent water. Thus, Tonto Creek is as low in elevation and, accordingly, as fertile as a trout stream in the White Mountains can be.

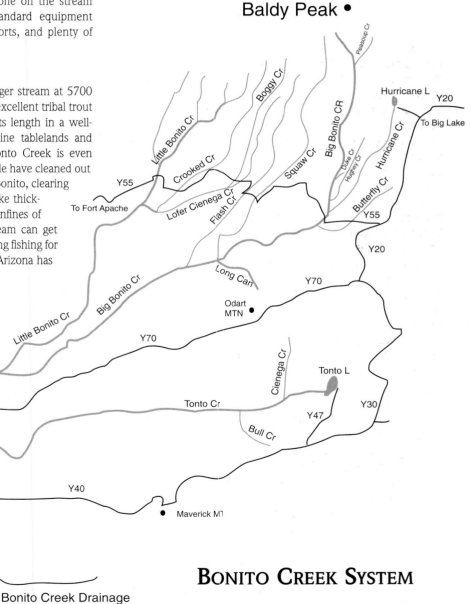

BONITO CREEK SYSTEM

Bonito Creek Drainage

12. BLACK RIVER SYSTEM

Name:	Black River
Location:	Apache-Sitgreaves National Forest, Apache and Graham Counties, Arizona
Maps:	Apache-Sitgreaves National Forest Visitors Map, USGS 1:100,000 series, Nutrioso
Elevation:	7000-5000 feet
Average Volume:	150 cfs
Length:	115 miles, below the confluence of East and West Forks
Best Times:	April, May, September-November
Fish Species:	Brown trout, Apache trout, rainbow trout, Sonoran sucker, longfin dace, smallmouth bass, channel catfish
Fishable Tributaries:	Turkey Creek, Paddy Creek, Ess Creek (plus an unnamed headwater branch), Pacheta Creek (plus two unnamed headwater branches), Bearwallow Creek, North Fork Bearwallow Creek, South Fork Bearwallow Creek Reservation Creek (plus upper and lower unnamed branches), Soldier Creek, Snake Creek, Conklin Creek (plus unnamed branch), Fish Creek, Double Cienega Creek (plus unnamed branch), Corduroy Creek, Bear Creek, Beaver Creek, Johns Canyon, Horton Creek, Willow Creek, Thomas Creek, Hannagan Creek, Hawksnest Canyon, Centerfire Creek, East Draw, Blow Draw, Boggy Creek, Wildcat Creek
West Fork Black River:	Headwater branch, Thompson Creek, Burro Creek, Stinky Creek, Hayground Creek, Home Creek, Horse Creek
East Fork Black River:	North Fork of East Fork, Merritt Draw, Spence Spring, Three Rivers Creek (plus unnamed branch), Boneyard Creek, unnamed spring, Coyote Creek, Open Draw, Deer Creek

The Black River system has more trout water than any other stream system in the Southwest, and some of the best. I'll review these waters from top to bottom, starting with the headwaters:

WEST FORK BLACK RIVER

The **West Fork** of the Black River heads on the southeast side of Mount Baldy, its headwaters forming in little meadows and canyons holding many small brown trout. **Burro Creek**, an upper tributary, plus the upper East Fork and the North Fork of the East Fork of the Black, used to drain an enormous wet meadow in the vicinity of today's artificially enhanced but reminiscent **Big, Crescent, and Basin lakes.** Trout could wend their way through seasonal sloughs filled by melted snow from Mount Baldy over a low basin connecting with the Lee Valley, a drainage of the Little Colorado River. In this respect, the entire meadow complex below the north and east slopes of the mountain could be thought of as a shallow, seasonal lake. Thus, Apache trout are native to the

upper Little Colorado headwaters, but not apparently to any of the other major tributaries of the Little Colorado which arise on the Mogollon Plateau. Decades of grazing, more grazing, and ditching have dried out the entire divide. Burro Creek, in particular, is now essentially a muddy wash with a number of stream improvement structures in its lower end but only a few mainly small browns in the water. It is mildly ironic to hunt for trout in a pool filled with both fancy stream-improvement structures and knee-deep silt. Results are almost always quite poor. Exclusionary fences, the farther from the stream the better, are without question the most effective stream improvement devices in this part of the world.

Other extreme headwaters of the West Fork are in far better shape. These include **Thompson Creek*** (closed within the White Mountain Apache Reservation, open within the Apache-Sitgreaves National Forest) plus one **unnamed, way-up tributary*** (on the reservation, closed). These waters flow through spruce forest mini-canyons and open meadows at the 9000-foot level through an undisturbed watershed, largely within the Apache Indian Reservation, and hold abundant populations of wild brown trout, six to a rare ten inches in size. Apache trout are now planted, as well. The best stretches are the meandering meadow reaches with undercut banks. Fishing is good here from July through September. The major access for this part of the Black River headwaters is from FR 113 and FR 116 connecting Big Lake and Reservation Lake. From the bridge crossing on FR 116 you can follow the essentially roadless **West Fork*** (the uppermost 4 miles of which is closed above the reservation boundary) either upstream to the just-mentioned smaller tributaries, or downstream to bigger water and bigger fish. The only other bridge across the river is at the other end, below the campground complex and right above the East Fork confluence. The 11-mile stretch of the West Fork from muddy Burro Creek to the East Fork is a roughly straight course through a gradually deepening and narrowing canyon. The upper reaches are open meadow with occasional patches of spruce and Douglas fir. Alder clumps occasionally line the banks, willow growth and narrowleaf cottonwood is scanty up high but abundant enough in the lower reaches to provide for a few of the beaver colonies that often create habitat for larger trout. There are few deep natural pools in the upper end, more below. All in all, the lower end is better habitat, with ponderosa pine and Douglas fir uplands yielding to a willow-cottonwood gallery in the canyon bottom. The ponds in the lower 5 miles or so provide the best chances for browns of 14 to 15 inches. Rainbows are stocked in the campground, but very few "take" in the stream.

Big Lake and nearby **Crescent Lake** (100 acres, 9040 feet) are very heavily fished. The campgrounds at Big Lake resemble a small town during summer months; the boat ramp is in nearly constant use—everything but parking meters. Things quiet down in October, when Phoenicians feel the cold wind and the cattle move in. The lake gets plenty of trout, about 400,000 a year—brookies, rainbows, even cutthroats. This is comparable to the entire stocking program spread over 1.6 million acres on the nearby White Mountain Apache Reservation. Crescent is just over a grassy knoll, barely out of sight. Noted for large brook char, this enhanced marsh has a boat launch but no campground. Nearby Basin Lake (30 acres), a smaller version of Crescent, holds brook char, also.

AZ G&F has marked the West Fork for watershed recovery and eventual restoration of Apache trout, closing most of the stream's upper reaches to cattle. Plants of Apaches have been made, rock-

and-wire gabions installed to protect the native trout from upstream incursion by browns, which still predominate both above and below the barriers. Similar structures are in place in **Stinky** and **Hayground creeks**, small side canyons of the West Fork reclaimed and reserved for Apache trout in the 1980s. Browns up to 14 inches have invaded here, also, Fishing is usually quite good in both of these canyon tributaries for small natives and the occasional large invader. Eight-mile-long **Home Creek**, arising just south of Big Lake and the lowermost tributary of the West Fork, has Apache trout, also, re-established in 1988, but fewer fish. Broad, shallow, and heavily grazed for many years, it sometimes dries out in its lower end. Most fish can be found in the four-mile reach below Conklin Spring, accessible via FS 24 from Big Lake. Finally, marshy **Horse Creek** empties into the West Fork just barely above the East-West Fork confluence. This tiny, overlooked rill holds a few browns and stray rainbows.

Of the many rainbow trout stocked in the West Fork Campground on the stream's lower end, a number wander downstream into the Black River mainstem which holds many wild rainbows. AZ G&F has for years reserved two- to three-hundred acres on the lower end of the West Fork, and there has always been excellent riparian habitat here. The water is slow and marshy in this reach, with beaver dams providing pools for a few larger trout.

Altogether, most of the fishing on the West Fork is done within the campground, itself, with a small but steady stream of fly-rodders attacking the stream at its upper end via the bridge at Burro Creek. Morning and evening fishing for the browns is good all summer long in the West Fork. If the water is slightly murky from the rains, but not muddy, the browns will often feed until noon—size 14 hares ear nymphs for the small ones, size 8 Woolly Buggers (green or black) for the 12- to 14-inchers. Weight your fly, or no bites.

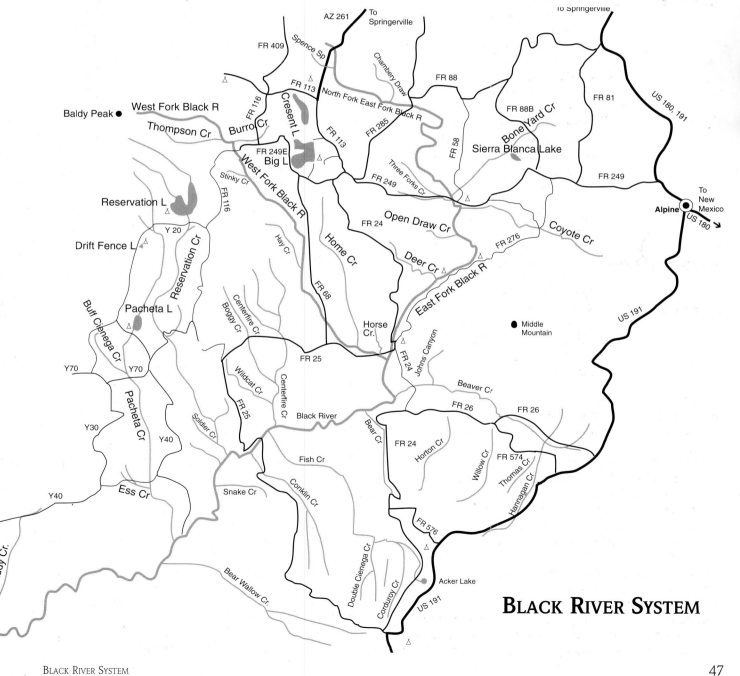

BLACK RIVER SYSTEM

EAST FORK BLACK RIVER

The **East Fork** of the Black River forms farther away from the mountain, from many spring branches at 9000 feet in the Big Lake meadows. Here it forms the **North Fork of the East Fork**, then falls into a canyon a few miles below Crosby Crossing, which deepens considerably below the **three forks**. From here it flows for some 26 miles before finally acquiring the West Fork and becoming the Black River proper. It is a larger stream than the West Fork and accordingly provides more fishing. The best reach is the roadless ten miles of water below Crosby Crossing (FR 285) and above Three Forks. Browns are found in the smaller water stretching five miles upstream, particularly in **Chambers Draw**, a meadow spring tributary which also holds rainbows, and in near-by **Merritt Draw** a mile or so above Crosby Crossing. The entire upper meadow region of the East Fork , ranging all the way to the Apache Reservation is dotted with cattle each summer, muddying the water and making fly fishing unworthy. It is only two to four miles below below Crosby Crossing, out of the major meadow, that the water clears and fishing becomes attractive. Browns predominate, with comparatively few fishermen to bother them.

The section between Three Forks and Diamond Rock Campground where the East Fork first forms its deep canyon, is fished more often but has bigger pools. Finally, a high-standard dirt road, FS 276, parallels the stream for its lower 10 miles, and during summer months this portion of the river bottom resembles a tent and RV city. I once worked an evening hatch, just off the road, and attracted a crowd of teenagers, who howled and giggled every time I hooked a fish. Traditionally, rainbow trout have been stocked along the campground areas, comprising most of the catch. Some of the rainbows have reproduced and remain, joined since 1995 by Apache trout planted yearly by AZG&F in an effort to reclaim more water for this threatened species. Wild browns from 7 to 20 inches, some even larger, are also present, though considerably harder to catch. Early morning nymphing in July and August, right at dawn, can generally produce one or two of 14 to 15 inches.

At the Three Forks, the North Fork of the East Fork joins with two other branches, small, spring-fed **Three Forks Creek**, a meadow stream holding browns and an occasional brook char, and the much larger, silty **Boneyard Creek**. Boneyard is also almost entirely a meadow stream, with a few scattered alder clumps. It was named near the turn of the century for starving cattle, and matters haven't changed greatly since—a shame, since this is potentially a superb stream. Wild browns to 14 inches and slightly smaller rainbows are found here, with the best fishing in the lower end and some good water also near the very head, where a few original Apache trout and Apache hybrids may still persist in two meadowy **upper branches**. During the summer, the water is often chocolate-colored, but when the water is not too dirty, browns can be caught near dawn or in evening, or immediately after a heavy shower. A headwater sub-tributary is dammed at 8400 feet to form muddy, pond-like **Sierra Blanca Lake**, heavily stocked with both cattle and AZ G&F rainbows. In 1998 I was told by Alpine Ranger District personnel that someone had recently shot a 25-inch brown with a .357 magnum handgun, near where the pond drains into the stream. Possibly this was out of frustration—some of the old cannibals simply can't be hooked. **Coyote Creek** empties into the East Fork a mile or so below Boneyard Creek. Though this heavily grazed open meadow stream

holds mostly dace, a few small browns are present in the lower mile or so. Once upon a time it was much better than this. If the watershed improves, it will be again.

Open Draw holds wild browns in its lower mile or so. Formed in a grazed meadow, it provides habitat only after entering a small canyon opening into the East Fork.

Usually dry, **Deer Creek** has a few spots of permanent water and marginal habitat for a few brown trout, including a very occasional uncatchable lunker in the roadside marsh where it meets the river.

BLACK RIVER (BELOW THE FORKS)

The **Black River mainstem**, 115 miles in total length, contains excellent trout fishing for 35 miles or so from the East-West Fork confluence to the mouth of Paddy Creek on the San Carlos/Fort Apache Indian Reservations, and good fishing for smallmouth bass and occasional trout some 30 miles beyond that, to the mouth of Bonito Creek. Browns and occasionally rainbows of up to 25 inches reside here, bass to three pounds, along with a myriad of Sonoran suckers. The smallmouths start to show up near Paddy Creek mouth, and hold in the still water, the trout claiming the deep holes below rapids. Below the Phelps Dodge diversion at White Crossing, the trout are much harder to find and the bass start to appear even in the rapids, dominating the fishery all the way into the Salt River, where they yield to the channel catfish. A good rule of thumb is that the bass start to predominate in the stream below 5600 feet, and the channel catfish become numerous below the 4500-foot mark. It is possible to catch all three species I'm guessing as far down as 5000 feet for trout, as far up as 5300 for catfish.

The water quality in Black River was exceptional in the 1960s but has declined somewhat since. The canyon is roadless in the Indian reservations, but many San Carlos and somewhat fewer White River tribal cattle keep the canyon bottom grazed and picked clean, which warms the water considerably. Nonetheless, the river still produces many, many fish, and a good share of them are still trout. You can fish the Black mainstem in the Apache Forest by hiking below FR 24 at Buffalo Crossing Campground in the Apache Forest for a mile or so and reach Black River where it first forms, but the best way to get at the upper Black River is from the Black Crossing, 12 miles below on FR 25. This road runs from US 191 south of Hannagan Meadow across the river and back around to the Buffalo Crossing on the East Fork. From the FR 25 bridge you can follow the canyon bottom either upstream to the forks, or downstream. If you go downstream more than six miles below the bridge, you need prior permission from the White Mountain Apache Tribe in Whiteriver, Arizona and the San Carlos Apache Tribe in San Carlos, AZ to cross into the reservation lands. The Black River forms the boundary between the two reservations. After you get your permits, you can follow as far downstream as you wish, as long as you plan on hiking out of the canyon and meeting a vehicle somewhere. The reservation portion of the canyon is quite remote, with no facilities, and with far fewer visitors than the national forest. The only easy road accesses are, first, at Black Crossing, way downstream 50 miles below the Apache Forest boundary and just a couple of miles above the confluence of the White and Black rivers, via tribal R9 out of Whiteriver; and also the Phelps Dodge pump station accessible from Point of Pines on the San Carlos Reservation via tribal road 2000. There is also

4-wheel-drive access to the canyon from Whiteriver via reservation roads number 70, 40, and 22. I tried one of them a while back in my '64 Valiant, didn't make it to the river, and I almost punched a hole in my oil pan. You need topo maps for these trips.

The bottom of the middle to lower Black River carries a six-inch or so layer of silt, a reminder of the fact that during the late 1960s the Prieto Plateau above the river was one of the heavier logging districts in the entire national forest system. The best areas to fish are immediately below the numerous rapids in the middle river, which keep the bottom swept clean. Some of these areas also contain the major spawning gravels, the scarcity of which is probably a limiting factor for trout populations.

Beaver Creek, a major tributary of the Black River, is the first stream to join the mainstem below the forks, forming on the Prieto Plateau just below 9000-foot Middle Mountain. The stream forms and flows for several miles through an open meadow called the Round Valley before passing the Sprucedale ranchstead and descending into its own mini-canyon and merging with the wild canyon of the Black River. The upper stream is open and cattle-prone, with hedged alders forming occasional patches of shade over the water, which is often muddy. Gamefish populations consist of wild browns and a very occasional original-strain Apache trout; fishing is best after the summer rains when the water is slightly discolored, and on overcast days. During such times the browns feed actively. Good evening hatches occur here in July and August.

Beaver Creek also has four tributaries of different character. All except Johns Creek and Hannagan Creek are dry at the mouth, and all are small, with wild browns and/or Apache trout populations. **Hannagan Creek,** the uppermost, has been reclaimed by the Apache trout. This is a tiny gem of a stream, easily accessible from FR 574 and the Coronado Trail (US 191). A small stock impoundment right alongside the Coronado Trail just south of Hannagan Meadow often holds several good-sized Apaches, even when the tiny creek below has all but disappeared—and no one notices them. **Thomas Creek**, entering Beaver Creek from the south just below Hannagan Creek, is generally dry and has precious few fish. I once did see a trout-form dart for cover at the stream's very head, but have never caught one here. **Willow Creek**, formed by a series of reliable springs below FR 564, flows through the timber at 8000 feet and holds browns in a three-mile reach before drying up above the FS 26 road crossing just south of its mouth into Beaver Creek. **Horton Creek**, just to the west, dries up also, becoming a dry gulch where FS 26 crosses it. It holds a few fish, including wild browns, in a two-mile stretch reachable by a hike upstream from the road. **Johns Creek** and **Hawksnest Canyon** hold mainly dace but also an occasional brown. The water quality in all these small tributaries is generally very good, much better than Beaver Creek.

The best holes in Beaver are down in the gorge below FR 24 where the stream joins the Black River. Two miles below this is the mouth of **Bear Creek**, small in flow but high in quality. Bear Creek receives its cold, clean water from a good set of springs 3 miles above, and holds a supply of healthy wild brown trout. Hard to fish because of willow and alder cover, the creek's undercut banks hold browns of up to 15 inches.

Several other tributaries of the Black River entering below Bear Creek contain native Apache trout, most re-introduced by the Arizona Game and Fish Department over the past several years.

These include south-flowing **Centerfire Creek**, entering the Black River from the north. Near its very head this small stream has two trout-filled tributaries joining it right at the FR 25 crossing. **East Draw** enters right at the culvert in a tree-rimmed meadow near the West Fork and Buffalo Crossing campgrounds. **Blow Draw** enters the left fork a short ways above. The forks of Centerfire are very tiny here, and so are the trout, but you can catch one or two of them with little trouble, just to see what Arizona's true natives look like. Centerfire has a good deal more water farther downstream, where its canyon joins the Black River, and browns predominate here, some of them to 15 inches. Medium-sized sub-tributary **Boggy Creek** crosses FS 25 a couple of miles to the west of the Centerfire culvert, and it has Apache trout that may approach 14 inches, along with cow pies, buzzing flies, beaver dams, and alder thickets, joining Centerfire just below the stream's upper meadow. **Wildcat Creek** is the next stream crossing FS 25, just east of the Apache reservation boundary, but it is only a dry gully where the road meets it. To find Apache trout you'll have to travel downstream half a mile or so. Like the previous two, it's a meadow stream above, falling into a dark canyon where it, too, joins Centerfire Creek. The mouths and lower end of all these streams are not fished very often, accessible only by foot, and are very good brown-trout water.

Fish Creek, on the other side of the river and reached by a different system of roads, is 13 miles long and accessible only by trail in its middle and lower reaches. This is arguably the best small trout stream in the Apache-Sitgreaves National Forest, and one of the best in the state. You will find many Apache and a few brown trout here, with large browns especially present in the twisting lower canyon, in hole after hole. In the open, meadow-rimmed headwaters, a number of small tributaries also support wild Apache trout populations. **Corduroy Creek** and **Double Cienega Creek** pour in near the head of the stream. Double Cienega forks at its head, each fork holding Apaches. Just to the east, across a low divide from Hannagan Meadow, tiny, acre-sized **Ackre Lake**, way up at 8850 feet, holds exotic arctic grayling. Some of these actually spawn in the insect-sized rivulet which forms the pond itself and which drains into uppermost Fish Creek. Some of the grayling in the pond grow to 15 inches, and if it's a state record your after, your best bet might be here, probably in the fall. After all, there are only two other spots in the state (Bear Canyon and Lee Valley reservoirs) where arctic grayling exist.

Just downstream from Fish Creek mouth and the FR 25 bridge, **Conklin Creek** is steep and small but live, holding wild Apache trout. It forks 2 miles above the Black River in heavy Douglas fir and ponderosa pine timber, and the forks hold Apaches, also. Often dry near its mouth, its flow is interrupted by dry reaches in early summer and late fall.

Reservation Creek, entering the Black River from the north, is far colder than the Black River where the two meet; the creek forms at an elevation of over 10,000 feet on the southwest slope of Mt. Baldy and flows south through the White Mountain Apache Reservation for 15 miles before rushing into the Black, at about 6800 feet. This is a superb, good-sized stream of about 15 cfs, holding brook char in its upper reaches and a mixed population of Apache x rainbow hybrids and browns of up to five pounds in its lower end. It has to be included on any list of "bests" in the state. A small dam at its upper end forms 280-acre, 9040-ft. spring and fall hotspot

Reservation Lake, full of brookies and rainbows, plus holdover browns of 10 pounds or better. The lake has a store and boat rental. The dam and campground areas of the lake are the only portion of the Reservation Creek watershed with public vehicle access. Most of the steep, whitewater middle and lower reaches accessible by foot seldom see anglers. The headwaters, closed above and open to fishing below the lake, hold many wet meadow reaches resembling Ord and Bear Cienega creeks on the other flank of Baldy. In summer the hillsides and streambanks come alive with shrub cinquefoil, flowering buckwheat, evening primrose, columbines, monkey flowers, and countless other forms. This long, narrow watershed contains tributary **Deep Cienega,** and a **small, unnamed branch*** above the west arm of Reservation Lake and holding brook char.

The lower 5 miles of the stream, just above Black River, hold Apache trout and some tremendous browns. I've seen fish of up to 6 pounds come out of this stream and its icy, waist-deep pools. In this stretch, tumbling **Soldier Creek** enters the Reservation Creek from the north. Noted for its original, unmolested population of pure-strain Apache trout, the stream forms all at once at Soldier Springs on the Fort Apache Reservation, then passes into the Apache Forest, flowing for about a mile and a half, joining Reservation Creek a couple of miles above the Black River. The fish in the stream have an odd, crimson tint, and are mostly small. The lower stream has many falls, is hidden in deep Douglas-fir shade, and in places is almost buried in willows. These same highly colored Apache trout can also can be found in Reservation Creek itself near Soldier Creek mouth, where another **small trickle** enters the creek, just above Soldier, and also has a few Apaches.

Two miles below Reservation Creek, **Snake Creek** enters from the southeast at 6600 feet. This is yet another small, steep Black River tributary holding wild Apache trout in about three miles of flow. You reach it at its mouth by hiking down the Black River and fishing up the stream, which is almost completely overlooked. While few people forsake the Black River to ascend the fair-sized Reservation Creek, almost no one takes a second look at this very good little stream.

Pacheta Creek, another superb tributary, is a sort of twin to Reservation Creek, similar in size, wilder, slightly lower in elevation (9200-6500 feet), more isolated, and possibly even better fishing. The Mt. Baldy headwaters, including a couple of tiny, **unnamed tributaries**, are cienega- and meadow-like and hold brook char, while the middle and lower reaches hold mainly browns, including some trophies that run 20 to 25 inches. The stream is 17 miles long, all in the reservation. I've never seen anyone fishing in roadside Pacheta Cienega, you can't even see the water. I don't stop here often mainly because it is just too easy to catch six-inch brookies and eight-inch browns almost everywhere you walk.The only parts which really get fished are in the vicinity of the **Pacheta Lake**, a 65-acre catch-and-release trophy brown-trout water dammed at 8200 feet, and at the old road crossing near the former lumber camp of Maverick a few miles downstream. Like several of the Mogollon Rim lakes 100 miles to the west, Pacheta Lake has many golden shiners, which provide food for the larger fish. Rainbows and Apache trout are also present in this lightly-used lake, now managed as a trophy, catch-and-release fishery. Springtime hotspot at 8900 feet and 16 acres, **Drift Fence Lake** sits beside the Reservation Lake-Whiteriver Road (tribal Y20). The lake is formed by an ephemeral tributary to Pacheta. Lots of rainbows are planted here, and a few brook char manage to sur-

vive the frequent winterkills. Middle tributary **Bluff Cienega** at Maverick has 2.5 miles of brown-trout habitat.

The lower end of Pacheta Creek is reached via the Pair O Dice Ranch turnoff, Y40. I've never seen anyone on this road, which branches off and dead-ends at Rattlesnake Point, shortly after crossing the creek. It also touches remote **Ess Creek**, about three miles in length, which gets constant, high-volume flow from headwater Ess Spring and its twin **headwater tributary**, and flows for about two miles before entering Pacheta 2.5 miles above the Black River and a mile below the Y40 road crossing. Chewed up by livestock and feral horses in the meadows below the spring, it nonetheless has for years provided superb fishing for wild browns in its lower reaches to those few who know about it. Below Ess, Pacheta Falls pours into a seldom-fished gorge inaccessible to cattle. The stretch between the falls and the river is my favorite piece of water in the state of Arizona.

Entering from the south a few miles below the mouth of Pacheta, **Bearwallow Creek** forms at 8500 feet elevation above the Mogollon Rim and flows for several miles through the mixed conifer forests of the Bearwallow Wilderness before entering the San Carlos Apache Reservation and then joining the Black River at the 6400-foot level. Apache *x* rainbow trout hybrids, mostly small, live both in moderate-sized Bearwallow and the tributary **North and South forks.** The total stream distance from the head of the North Fork to the Black River, is about 12 miles. Population levels are lower than average, and the upper reaches of the North Fork are well grazed.

Similar to Ess Creek, **Paddy Creek** is extremely steep, starting as a meadow spring along the Tonto Lake turnoff from Y40, then falling four miles into the Black River itself from Paddy Butte. A good population of wild browns survives in this extremely isolated, seldom-visited stream.

Turkey Creek flows from 7000 to 600 feet through the mid-elevation pine and juniper forests below the Seven Mile Ridge and Corn Creek Plateau. Its dry bed enters Black River a few miles below the mouth of Bonito Creek (see page 36). Very seldom fished, it is often dry below the Tribal Y40 road but is said to hold a few trout above, among beaver ponds. **Corn Creek**, just to the east, is even smaller, even more seldom visited. It contains a mile or two of small flow at 6700-7000 feet, dry at its mouth at 5300 feet, into Bonito Creek, not Black River. Nonetheless, I'm grouping it here with Turkey Creek, its twin. Fish are in it, including possibly a few trout near its head at 7000 feet. **Corn Creek Tank**, 5 acres at 6300 feet, holds warmwater fish, possibly a trout or two.

SAN CARLOS STOCK TANKS

In the southern headwaters of the Black River, the San Carlos Apache Reservation boasts dozens of small stock tanks scattered throughout the Natanes Mountains. These are planted with rainbow trout from time to time, and a number carry the trout over for several years. For the latest stocking schedules, you can reach the tribal headquarters at San Carlos Arizona. The two biggest permanent tanks, **Point of Pines Lake** (27 acres, 6400 feet) and **Seneca Lake** (25 acres, 5000 feet), always hold some trout. Seneca, reached via the Globe-Showlow Highway south of the Salt River bridge, is marginal. Point of Pines, reachable by dirt roads leading through the Natanes Mountains from San Carlos village, usually yields catches. Point of Pines drains into Eagle Creek (see the section on Eagle Creek, page 60).

13. LITTLE COLORADO RIVER SYSTEM

Name: Little Colorado River
Location: Apache-Sitgreaves National Forest, Apache and Graham Counties, Arizona
Maps: A-S NF Visitors Map; USGS 1:100,000 series, Nutrioso and Springerville editions
Elevation: 8000-5900 feet
Average Flow: Estimated at 10 cfs
Length of Fishing Water: 40 miles, 8700 elevation at Greer to 6500 feet elevation. below Springerville
Best Times: April, May, September, October
Fish Species: Brown trout, rainbow trout, Sonoran sucker, longfin dace,
Fishable Tributaries: Concho Creek (few trout), Silver Creek, Show Low Creek, Walnut Creek, Porter Creek (few trout), Walnut Creek (few trout), Carnero Creek (few trout), Mineral Creek* (closed), Coyote Creek, Morrison Creek, Mamie Creek, Nutrioso Creek, Rudd Creek, Benton Creek, Riggs Creek, Colter Creek, Augur Creek, Hulsey Creek, Paddy Creek, Water Canyon, South Fork Little Colorado, Fish Creek, Hall Creek, Rosie Creek (few trout), Benny Creek, Bunch Reservoir flowage, West Fork Little Colorado River (plus one headwater branch), East Fork Little Colorado River, Lee Valley Creek

The **Little Colorado River**, known mainly as a desert wash passing through Navajo-Hopi country, has an entirely different character where it forms in the high mountains of eastern Arizona. Here it begins as two forks on the northern slope of 11,400-foot Mount Baldy in a minuscule wilderness area in the Apache National Forest. Its upper reaches flow below an alpine meadow which in pre-Columbian times formed a network of cienegas circling Mt. Baldy's eastern flanks, allowing the native Apache trout to pass freely among the Black, White, and Little Colorado systems. Today, all that remains of these *cienegas* is a network of cow pastures and shallow, grassy reservoirs of various sizes, the largest being the 890-acre Sunrise and 500-acre Big Lake (in the White and Black River watershed, respectively). After leaving the meadows on the top of the White Mountains, the Little Colorado flows eastward through a basalt-ribbed canyon formed just downstream from Greer, Arizona, leaves the national forest boundary, then turns north passing through the small Mormon lumbering town of Springerville, and flows across the state, converting to an enormous Painted Desert wash and becoming part of the Grand Canyon complex some 400 miles from its Mount Baldy source. Just before emptying into the Colorado, it absorbs natural salts from an enormous spring under its bed. Many tons of salt pour into the Colorado River every day from this spot, changing the river's water.

Though trout inhabit the Little Colorado from the headwaters

down to the 6000-foot level 50 river miles away, fishing for them is feasible only above Springerville, 30 miles below the river's head on Mount Baldy. Here the Little Colorado is almost strictly a brown-trout stream. Rainbows are stocked heavily near Greer, but few seem able to compete. Spawning success is limited.

One of the best stretches of the Little Colorado River above Springerville is in the basalt canyon from Greer to the Apache National Forest boundary, and a few miles beyond. The water is often cloudy, either from early-season snow-melt, July rains, or late-season algae, but this enables you to stalk the abundant brown trout during the daylight hours, from May to October. The water volume is good, which means higher overall trout populations. There is one fisherman's parking lot provided by the state on FR 560 just downstream from the mouth of the South Fork, but private land blocks upstream fishing about a half mile above. The other access here is downstream, by foot, from Apache Forest land; the going can be difficult, but fishing here is worth the effort. The river is reachable from state highway 373, via Hall Creek bridge, or from **Bunch Reservoir** or **River Reservoir**, downstream. Bunch and River are two of the three so-called **Greer Lakes**, all lying at approximately 8300 feet just downstream from the resort village of Greer, Arizona. All three are small but hold large browns (up to 14 pounds in River Reservoir) and pan-sized stocked rainbows.

A few miles downstream from the forest boundary, the Little Colorado's stripped banks and side arroyos start to absorb abuse at a rapid rate, and water quality deteriorates accordingly. The best fishing below Springerville is in an un-prepossessing old irrigation impoundment called **Becker Lake**, built over a springhead right on the edge of town, just away from the river. Though the setting isn't scenic, the water is fine-looking. Special regulations include a closed season, something few Arizona waters have. It is good in the spring and fall for the usual rainbows and browns, of larger average size here because of the regs. The spring-fed lake remains clear most of the year.

All in all, the several upper branches of the Little Colorado provide highly variable fishing. **Hall Creek**, 7 miles long, enters just below Greer and holds a good supply of browns in the canyon on its lower end, and nearly as many in its upper narrows. You can fish down from the Greer Road (A373) and continue on to the Little Colorado River mouth. Here you'll find the best water on the Little Colorado, also. Wading, of course, is required, to waist-level in places. Fishing is spottier in the uppermost meadow near AZ 273 and the reservation boundary at 9200 feet, where a dam forms a seldom-photographed seasonal impoundment, **White Mountain Reservoir**, which lacks only water. Rainbows are planted here when feasible.

Benny and **Rosie creeks** hold some browns in beaver ponds in the vicinity of Greer. Rosie, the smaller, flows into Benny. It has a nice little spring but is nonetheless nearly unfishable in dry years. Benny forms a little canyon below the Greer Lakes, about 2 miles long, and here you can always find a few. **Fish Creek**, entering just below the mouth of Hall, is even smaller than Rosie, and is ditched dry from time to time in its upper reaches. The concept of in-stream flows hasn't yet arrived to this neck of the woods. Nearby **Carnero Creek** rises off 10,134-foot Greens Peak and flows northwards, almost straight down into the red and gold volcanic prairies stretching beneath the White Mountains. Much like Fish Creek, it is de-watered for irrigation, leaving trout habitat high and dry. For this purpose, also, it is dammed near its source at 9000 feet to form **Carnero Reservoir**, 65 acres, where rainbows are occasionally deposited.

The roadless, brushy **South Fork**, 8 miles long, enters a mile below the Apache Forest boundary; it holds only browns, and, with its superb water quality can be an excellent stream in years of good precipitation. It is reachable at its mouth via FR 560, which branch-

es off AZ 260 and leads to a small picnic ground near the mouth of the stream. Fishing is fine along the stream above. A trail, FT 97, leads a mile or so up the canyon, then you scramble over the moss, logs, and mini-falls in the upper canyon. In the meadows on top lies **Mexican Hay Lake** at 8900 feet, mostly hay, 100 acres when full, 0 acres in recent years. Another stream, **Water Canyon**, enters the Little Colorado just below the mouth of the South Fork. Once filled

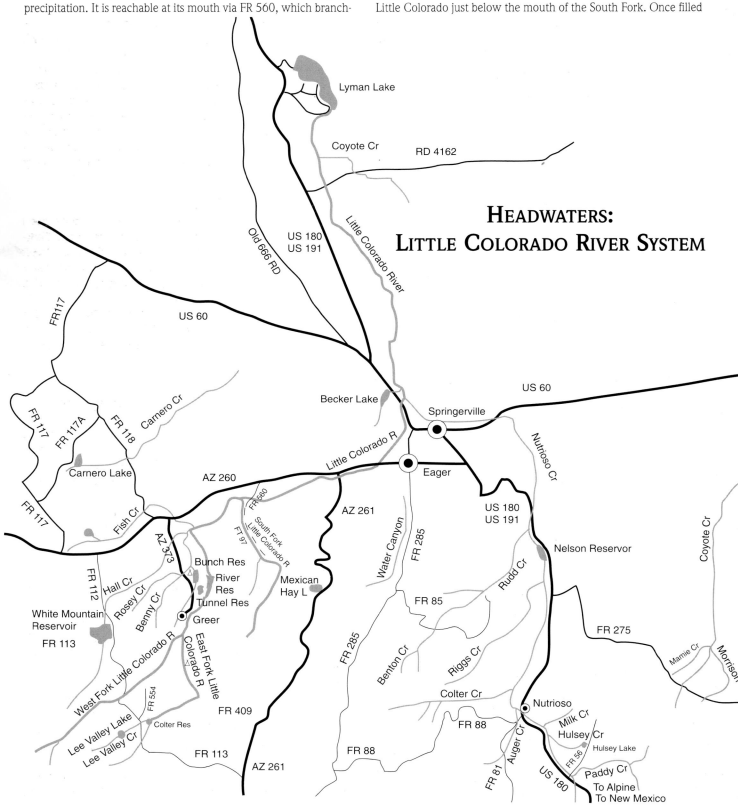

HEADWATERS:
LITTLE COLORADO RIVER SYSTEM

with native Apache trout and a popular local fishing destination, the water is now drawn so low for irrigation that only a few trout, if any, remain. Hay is the priority.

Above Greer the river forks; the water is smaller, but numerous meadow reaches provide undercut banks, and the fishing is far easier. Way up at the top of the Little Colorado, the good-sized **West Fork**, the fair-sized **East Fork,** and the micro **Lee Valley Creek** flow directly off Mount Baldy within the tiny, 7000-acre Mt. Baldy Wilderness, suitable for six-inch-high Daniel Boones and seven-inch-long brown trout. Here the 9000-foot West Fork and its **small branch** hold scads of the little wild browns in crystal-clear water, flowing over duckweed and watercress through open meadows. Immediately below Sheep Crossing the West Fork enters a small canyon offering rapids and pools, and the trout accordingly get bigger. The total length of fishing water is about 14 miles. The smaller, 10-mile East Fork also holds browns, plus a very few brook char in its upper end; it has more beaver ponds and marshes in its middle reaches. Farther down, it, too, falls into a small canyon two miles above its join with the West Fork, just above Greer. Lee Valley Creek flows from 9000 to 8000 feet; it has Apache trout above flawless 35-acre **Lee Valley Lake,** which holds brook char, Apache trout, and arctic grayling. A very few trout of any kind make their way below here through a heavily grazed meadow to tiny, unreliable **Coulter Reservoir** (0-30 acres, 9100 ft.), where the stream joins the East Fork.

Farther to the east in much drier country, **Coyote Creek** forms on the north slope of fire-scarred,10,900-foot-high but relatively waterless Escudilla Mountain, detours a couple of miles into New Mexico, then dries out and winds through the rabbitbrush mesas north of the Apache National Forest, finally draining into the Little Colorado twelve miles north of Springerville. Right under Escudilla at the 9000-foot level, ice-cold permanent tributaries **Morrison and Mamie creeks,** lined with blue spruce, bracken ferns, alders, and occasional elderberry shrubs, have truly tiny flows but nonetheless provide habitat for pure-strain Apache trout, re-introduced here in the early 1980s. During wet years these fish move well down into Coyote Creek itself, the uppermost 6 miles of which hold slightly larger Apaches in a few scattered beaver pools.

Nutrioso Creek, another, much larger Escudilla Mountain drainage, is about 25 miles long. Muddy and degraded in its lower reaches below 60-acre, 7450-foot **Nelson Reservoir** and quite small above, it flows into the Little Colorado just outside the Springerville town limits. The many little beaver ponds in the lower end, formed of willows, grass, and odd wattles (no cottonwoods here), provide for a very rare rainbow trout specimen. The rabbitbrush barrens surrounding the creek bed tell you that this stream has been truly hammered by cattle for many decades, and the fishing shows it. Nelson Reservoir itself holds a few brown trout, plus brook char and many rainbows, the latter two also found in tributary **Rudd Creek** entering the Nutrioso just below the dam. Rudd Creek also has wild rainbows farther up, for a total of 4 miles of habitat. A ranch here was purchased in the early 1990s using state lottery gambling dollars. The result is a Nature Conservancy-type preserve which will help the creek's trout recoup some of their own losses. Upper sub-tributary **Benton Creek** has three miles of rainbows and many cows. Fishing is slow. At the top of the drainage, **Augur Creek** forms on Noble Mountain and provides extremely marginal fishing for scattered small rainbows in 4 miles of public water before joining Nutrioso in Nutrioso village. The erosion here from logging, compounded yet again by cows, has filled the stream with sand and muck and virtually destroyed the already limited fishery.

Other Nutrioso tributaries **Riggs Creek** and **Colter Creek,** each about three miles long, pour in just below Augur, which they also resemble. You'll have any of these poor streams to yourself, for good reason. Higher up yet, and on the better side of US 180, **Paddy Creek** is a Nutrioso tributary in the heavy timber on Escudilla's western flank. This is extremely small but in a better-managed grazing allotment and holds scads of tiny, wild rainbow trout all the way up to **Toolbox Draw,** some of these fish still contain Apache-era genes. Nearby **Hulsey Creek** flows through its heavily stocked namesake reservoir, the creek holding small rainbows—sometimes, when there's water. Scenic, 3-acre **Hulsey Lake** yields many rainbow catchables at 8620 feet and is popular with the locals, keeping them away from the fragile streams.

CONCHO WATERSHED

Below Lyman Reservoir, the muddy Little Colorado cannot support trout. In the mid-elevation prairie near Snowflake, the unlikely-looking but surprising Concho drainage enters. **Concho Creek and Reservoir** are extremely mossy at 6000 feet, but powerplant trout seem to do reasonably well here, at least in the 60-acre lake. Subdivisions lie above the west bank.

Northwest of Greer, high-elevation **Mineral Creek***, its 2.5 miles closed to fishing for now by AZ G&F, holds pure-strain Apache trout before flowing north into the prairie and drying out above Concho Creek.

SILVER CREEK SYSTEM

Farther downstream, the Silver Creek system enters the Little Colorado in the bleak plains just above Holbrook. **Silver Creek,** formed at a beautiful springs now the site of a state fish facility, flows for about 13 miles at the 6000-foot level before muddying, drying, and draining into the Little Colorado. The stream was named by homesteaders for its gliding, clear, silvery-blue water, formed by limestone springs. This is the only major trout stream in the state not arising within a national forest, national park, or Indian reservation, and its fate in recent years is instructive. When the 150,000-acre Bourdon Ranch was sold in the 1970s, developers immediately snatched up nearly the entire creek, and subdivisions offering "a piece of Arizona" popped up instantly; meanwhile, the silver stream itself, now a private recreational property, has turned a murky, dishwater gray.

The uppermost 3 miles of water were purchased by Arizona Game and Fish in 1979, and this stretch provides most of today's trout habitat and virtually all the public water. The uppermost half mile or so is used to rear Apache trout and is closed to fishing. Here headwater Silver Spring turns the barren Brown Wash into a water-filled wildlife haven, providing 3 cfs of crystal flow, welling up out of the ground into a deep pool, while another spring a few hundred yards below provides about 1 cfs. The water emerges at 59 degrees, but climbs to 65 degrees within a few yards. There is virtually no shade here, except for the tall rushes giving the whole watercourse a marshy appearance—beaver are forced to climb up the banks and find juniper trees for their cuttings. Below the closed area, rainbows can be caught through the summer all the way down to the threatening "Keep Out" signs just below the Bourdon Ranch Road crossing. The trout themselves seem to have obeyed the signs, for most of the fishing peters out below the crossing.

A small number of rainbows do survive at 80-acre **White Mountain Lake** (private), formed by the creek four miles below the hatchery. There is no shady canyon here and at 5950 feet, the water heats up in the summer sun, ending most of the trout fishing in the waters below the dam.

One of Silver Creek's downstream tributaries, **Show Low Creek,** holds scattered rainbow trout in the upper end of its own 35-mile murky flow. This sluggish stream makes its way from the very edge of the Mogollon Rim west of Lakeside to 140-acre, 6300-foot **Fools Hollow Lake**, 4 miles below the now-unlovely resort town of Show Low. Its dry bed then continues on for many miles, joining Silver Creek south of Taylor, Arizona. Fools Hollow holds catfish, largemouth bass, walleye, and brown trout. Upstream reservoir **Show Low Lake**, 100 acres and deep, holds rainbows, browns, plus walleyes, etc. on the outskirts of Show Low at 6540 feet. The best fishing in the creek is immediately above the lake, on forest land protected (for now) from the subdivisions.

Show Low Creek also has a number of sluggish, turbid tributaries farther upstream. One of them, **Walnut Creek**, originates at 6900 feet at 18-acre **Woodland Lake**, then flows into 80-acre, 6700-foot **Rainbow Lake.** This little stream holds a surprising number of nice rainbow trout in its lower reaches, probably Rainbow Lake migrants. Woodland Lake is part of a rare county park, holding good-sized, tasty channel catfish, less numerous bass, plus rainbow and brown trout. Below Woodland Lake, access is a problem for most of the creek and nearly all of Rainbow Lake, once a beauty spot photographed in *Arizona Highways* magazine and now a private resort and summer home property.

Another Show Low tributary, **Porter Creek** drains 80-acre **Scott Reservoir** at 6700 feet and flows into the outskirts of Lakeside, Arizona. The reservoir has brown and rainbow trout. The creek is full of litter, old tires, and looks muddy. **Billy Creek** flows from Pinetop to Lakeside and is a good match for Porter—it looks Billy-ish. The water in both Porter and Billy creeks is still clean enough for a few rainbow trout.

FLAGSTAFF AREA

Two 7000-foot reservoirs high in the pines on the Mogollon Plateau south of Flagstaff also hold trout year round. **Ashurst Lake**, 160 acres at 7100 feet, is on Coconino National Forest Road 82E and is heavily stocked with rainbows. There used to be a lot of brook char in this lake, and a few still turn up occasionally. **Kinnikinick Lake,** 125 acres at 7040 feet, is farther from Flagstaff, harder to reach on rougher forest roads 124 and 82, and holds slightly bigger trout, including browns. In theory, at least, both of these ponds drain into the Little Colorado.

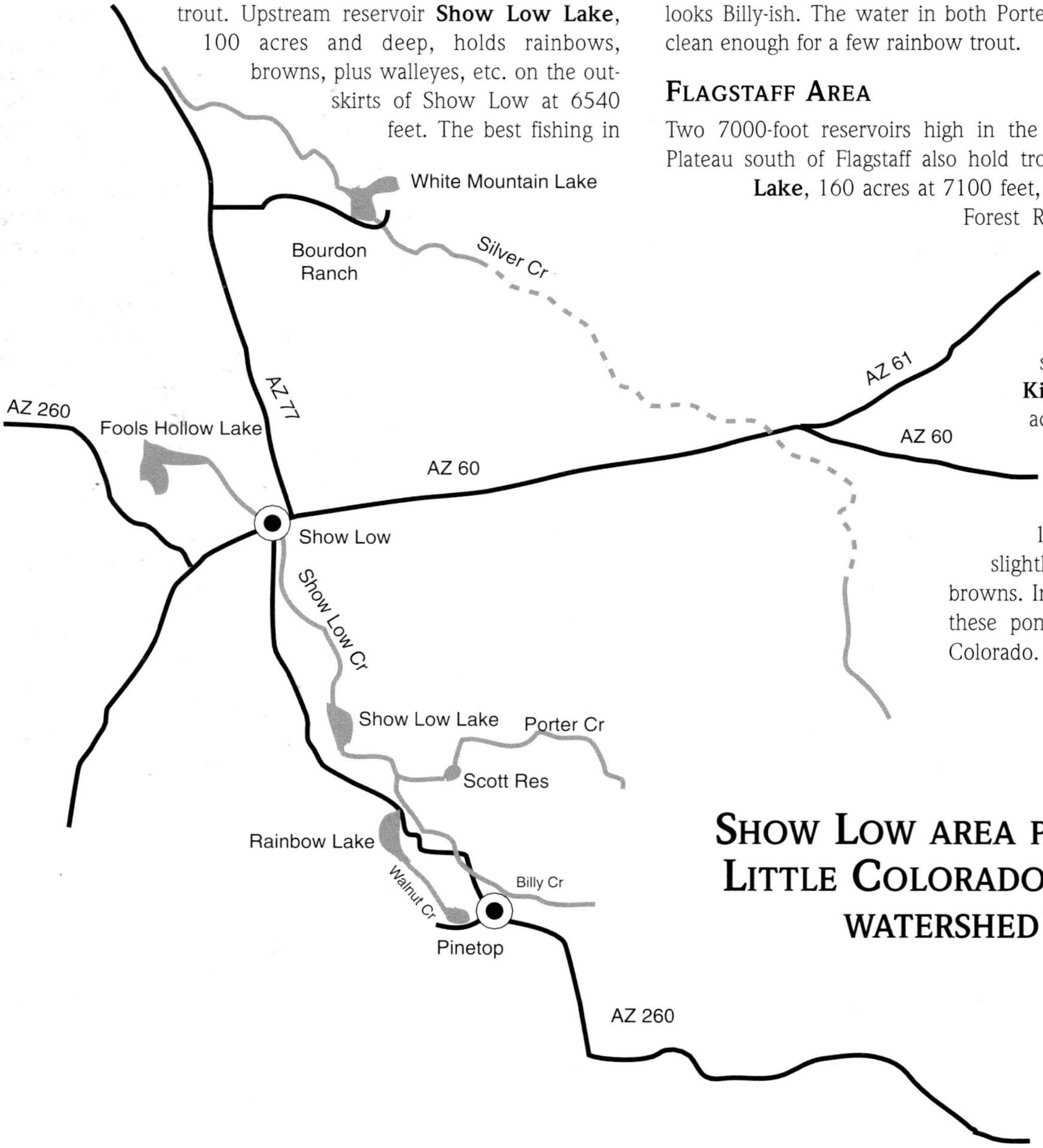

White Mountain Lake

Bourdon Ranch

Silver Cr

AZ 77

AZ 61

AZ 260

Fools Hollow Lake

AZ 60

AZ 60

Show Low

Show Low Cr

Porter Cr

Show Low Lake

Scott Res

Rainbow Lake

Billy Cr

Walnut Cr

Pinetop

AZ 260

SHOW LOW AREA PART OF LITTLE COLORADO RIVER WATERSHED

54

14. SAN FRANCISCO RIVER SYSTEM

Name: Upper San Francisco River
Location: Apache-Sitgreaves National Forest, Apache and Graham Counties
Maps: Apache -Sitgreaves NF Visitors Map, USGS 1:100,000 series Nutrioso edition
Elevation: 8300-7700 feet (3200 feet at its confluence with the Gila River)
Fishable Length: 15 miles above the New Mexico state line
Average Flow Volume: 15 cfs below Luna Lake (70 cfs at Gila River confluence)
Best Times: April, May, September-November
Fish Species: Brown trout, rainbow trout, Sonoran sucker, desert sucker, speckled dace, channel catfish
Trout-bearing Tributaries: Turkey Creek, Stone Creek (very few trout), Romero Creek, (tributary of New Mexico's Trout Creek), several others in New Mexico

The **San Francisco River** is a major Gila River tributary, rising beneath 10,900-foot Escudilla Mountain and gaining its first flow at 8300 feet just west of Alpine, Arizona, flowing eastwards into New Mexico fifteen miles downstream, then cutting southwards through the San Francisco Mountains and other smaller ranges for roughly 100 miles before re-entering Arizona in a wild, semi-desert box canyon where it receives the flow of the Blue River. After passing through yet another range and another, true-desert box canyon, it pours into the Gila a short ways above the mouth of Eagle Creek. Of its roughly 150-mile total length, only for its first fifteen miles above the state line can it be classified as an Arizona trout stream. Most of the remaining trout disappear below the village of Reserve, New Mexico, thirty river miles or so below the state line. The "Frisco" is marginal water above its one and only impoundment, 75-acre, 7900-foot **Luna Lake** east of Luna, and only slightly better below. Above Luna Lake the river is almost entirely on private land; the 5-mile stretch between Alpine and the lake is quite muddy and nasty-looking, with a black silty bottom. A mile or two upstream from Alpine it looks better, and there are a couple of private ranch ponds offering fee fishing, while brook and rainbow trout can be found on a brief stretch of Apache Forest land on uppermost tributary **Turkey Creek**, running clear and clean right alongside U.S.

Highway 180. This grassy stream is so small as to escape everyone's notice—both small brookies and slightly larger rainbow trout hiding below undercut meadow banks know it very well, however, at least during wet years.

Below Luna Lake and its Forest Service campgrounds, the river enters a roadless canyon offering few natural campsites, occasional rapid water, and holes which harbor rainbows of up to 15 inches, along with swarms of suckers. The Luna Lake outflow is soupy during summer heat, but streamside sedges filter it along the way. Even though it flows way up here at 7700 to 8000 feet, the river is never actually clean and not always cold, but it does clear a bit in the fall. It is virtually unfished, most visitors tending to concentrate on the stocker rainbows, brook, and occasional generic cutthroat trout deposited all summer long into Luna Lake. There is a fishing derby at the lake in August, very popular. Boats can be rented in summer, and there are two busy campgrounds just above the north shore.

Often you can do better in the stream below than in the lake when fishing for wild, unstocked rainbow trout. Except for a precious few in the Eagle Creek system, there are no browns in the entire San Francisco watershed.

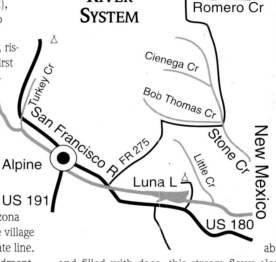

Stone Creek falls eight miles into the San Francisco River from the south slopes of Escudilla, crossing into New Mexico two miles above its mouth. Silty and filled with dace, this stream flows along banks lined almost entirely with Bermuda grass and small clumps of decades-old alder bushes, the latter having been kept from growing into trees by heavy summer grazing for decades. Rainbows are reportedly found here, but I have never seen one. If you want to wander the banks of this abused little stream, be prepared to sink into mud and quicksand. Nearby **Little Creek** should have trout, also, but doesn't seem to, either. Romero Lake and Creek hold very few rainbow trout if you ever find yourself on the far side of the mountain.

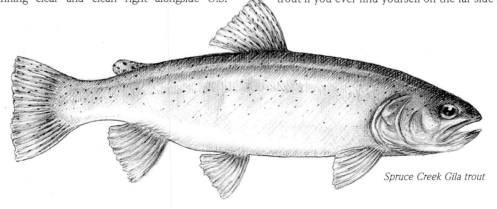

Spruce Creek Gila trout

15. Blue River System

Name: Blue River

Location: Blue Range Primitive Area, Apache-Sitgreaves National Forest, Apache and Graham Counties, Arizona, Dry Blue RARE II roadless area, Gila National Forest, Catron County, New Mexico

Maps: Gila National Forest, Apache-Sitgreaves National Forest Visitors Maps, USGS 1:100,000 series, Clifton edition

Elevation: 7000-3900 feet

Length: 75 miles

Average Flow Volume: 51 cfs, varies greatly

Best Times: April, May, September-November

Fish Species: Brown trout, rainbow trout, Sonoran sucker, desert sucker, speckled dace, loach minnow, channel catfish

Trout-bearing Tributaries: Thomas Creek (very few trout), Rosensock Creek (very few), Strayhorse Creek, Raspberry Creek, McKittrick Creek (few trout), KP Creek (plus headwater branch, middle unnamed tributary, Blue Lookout tributary), Grant Creek (plus upper tributary and Long Cienega Creek, with few trout), Lamphier Canyon, Foote Creek, Right Fork, Foote Creek, Bush Creek, Dry Blue Creek, Pace Creek, Campbell Blue Creek, Castle Creek, Buckalou Creek, Coleman Creek, Cienega Creek

Mountain ranges and rivers are not aware of longitudinal medians, and the eastern boundary of Arizona's Mogollon Rim and Blue Range move seamlessly into the state of New Mexico near the 109th west parallel.

The 75-mile-long **Blue River**, forming on the Mogollon Rim and flowing through the entire length of the Blue Range, is an Arizona stream, but it makes a slight detour out of the state. It starts off in Arizona as **Campbell Blue Creek** on the flank of Middle Mountain, flowing through a seam in the upper Blue Range. After entering New Mexico, Campbell Blue acquires the flow of two New Mexico tributaries, **Dry Blue** and **Pace Creeks**, both of which have limited numbers of stream-born brown trout. Here it becomes the Blue River proper before leaving the state. The Blue cuts deeply into the eastern end of the Mogollon Rim, draining the Prieto Plateau, the Blue Range, and the western San Francisco Mountains. Its upper basin is deeply eroded all around, yet surrounded by shaggy-topped, richly forested ridges and rounded peaks. Its canyon topography is quite a bit like the Sierra Ancha range far to the west, northeast of Phoenix. The stream itself very much resembles Eagle Creek, a former Gila trout habitat draining the Mogollon Rim just a few miles away. In its basic character it is a lower-elevation desert stream, ranging from 6500 to 3900 feet, of extremely high fertility.

The chief drawback to the mild climate here has been long-standing year-round grazing, with several abandoned ranchsteads lining the lower rivercourse; grazing has been particularly brutal in this steep watershed, and the associated upland erosion and downstream water quality problems are something quite familiar to those who look for trout in the nearby Gila National Forest. On balance, it is still a fair stream holding wild browns and some rainbows in its upper 50 miles; its uppermost section has smaller flow and spotty fishing. Parts of the upper river dry up occasionally, but populations always rebound in wet years. I've caught many nice trout in these same upper reaches, particularly in the Jackson Box section (in Arizona), which always has a decent amount of water. In hot summer months the partial sub-surface flow of the upper river actually helps keep the water cool. The upper stream also has scattered groves of cottonwoods and willow banks. Beaver ponds provide refuge in the stream reaches five miles or so below the upper box section. Closed to grazing to protect loach minnow populations in the late 1990s and no longer stocked, the river is making a very gradual return to gallery forest. Sycamore sprigs now appear in the lower canyon. I haven't noticed any decline in the fishing despite the suspended stocking and dry years in 1995 and 1996.

After acquiring several tributaries, the Blue produces slightly better fishing in the roadless lower section passing through the Blue Range Primitive Area; it appears to become too warm for trout in the semi-desert below Pigeon Creek, twenty miles north of its mouth into the San Francisco River, which is at this lower elevation a desert stream passing below Morenci, Arizona. Charged with the debris-filled flow of the Blue, the San Francisco nearly wiped out the nearby town of Clifton, Arizona in late winter of 1983, and the town has never been the same since. The Blue also tore out a concrete bridge 25 feet above the streambed in Blue Box, just above the roadless section of the primitive area. Even though the area is roadless and largely trail-less, erosion rates here are many times the natural baseline. Interestingly enough, prevention of erosion and protection of stream courses, along with protection of the timber supply, were the original purpose for the creation of the Apache Forest Reserve around the turn of the century.

The Blue has sediment and water temperature problems, but also a long growing season. When conditions are right, the fish grow very fast. I've managed to catch a fair number of 14- to 16-inch browns and rainbows over the years, in April, May, September, and October. I don't generally fish here during the summer, but it is possible to do so. The heat in the Blue Valley, lying at a south-inclining 5000 to 6000 feet, is oppressive in the summer, but the fish seem to come to life after the daily late July and August rains. The browns, in particular, feed during the day if the water clouds up a bit, which it does very easily after rain. As is the case on so many other Arizona streams, overcast conditions make these fish bolder, also. A rainy, overcast spell in early May a few years ago produced phenomenal fishing within the primitive area between Raspberry and Strayhorse Creek mouths, with 12- to 16-inch rainbows striking immediately in every pool, along with many smaller fish. The scene repeated itself in October. I've also seen the larger pools filled with big rainbow trout during spawning time in early April, also ready to strike at any lure. As usual, there were no other fishermen on the entire river on any of those days. Upper Blue is accessible by FR 281, a

23-mile dirt road south of Luna Lake near Alpine, Arizona, which extends along the Blue Valley for another 25 miles or so before dead-ending just below the mouth of KP Creek. Below here the river is roadless all the way down to a jeep crossing just above the desert-like mouth of Pigeon Creek, some 20 stream miles away. I generally expect to see three or four cars a day on the lower end of the one road, mostly rancher folk in their elongated pick-ups. Another, slightly rougher dirt road, FR 567, descends into the canyon from Hannagan Meadow on the Coronado Trail (US 191), meeting 281 at the upper river. Only once have I seen others fishing the Blue, two stocky college students from Phoenix astounded to have found brown trout in a pool beside the road.

Like many other trout streams in the *Sierra del Gila* flowing at 6000 feet or less, the Blue seems unfit for trout at first glance, with its constantly gliding schools of suckers in the deep pools and slower currents, dace in the shallows, and not a trout in sight. Appearances can be deceiving, however. Trout are there. Seldom can I see the trout in the lower Blue, until one darts out from under a rock ledge to seize a weighted nymph twitched just off the bottom. This is precisely the way the Middle Fork of the Gila River in neighboring New Mexico looks, also. In fact, a 20-year Forest Service employee stationed at the Gila Visitors Center once told me that right after he arrived from Idaho he took a fishing pole down to that small river and started casting to a school of 15-inch fish. Frustrated by his lack of success, he soon realized that they were all suckers, 20 or more of them. He put his pole away and never fished the Gila again. That was a mistake. The Middle Fork and the Blue hold just as many trout as the Idaho waters of similar size he had grown used to.

Besides the 50 trout-bearing miles of the mainstem, Blue drainage holds by my count no fewer than 20 trout-bearing tributaries and sub-tributaries. Some of these offer excellent fishing in wet years; many are too degraded and/or too small to be of great general interest. Fish any one of them in a wet year and you might make plans to return. If you return in a dry year, you might find that the stream is no longer there. All of these streams, even the main Blue River above the FR 567 crossing, can dry up completely for varying stretches during some summers. The standing pools, cooled by the stream's sub-surface flow, will still support small numbers of surviving trout. Reproduction occurs each spring in spite of these

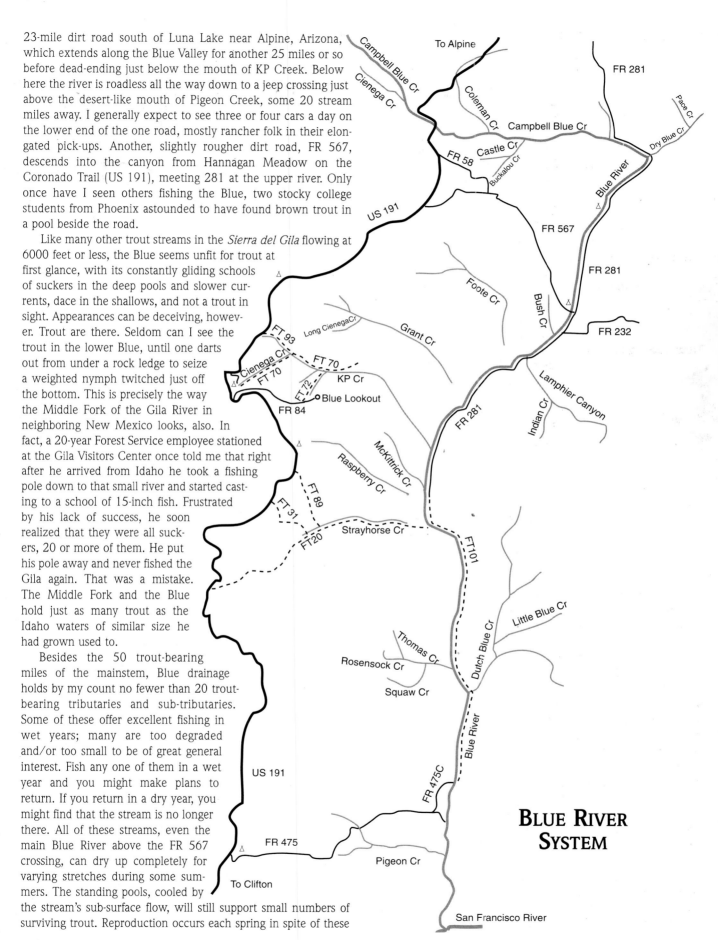

BLUE RIVER
SYSTEM

constraints, in nearly all of the waters and sub-streams. Many of the uppermost tributaries still contain hybridized Arizona native trout.

Campbell Blue Creek, at the head of the Blue system, provides slow fishing up top, but the middle canyon section between Luce Ranch and the Coronado Trail provides fairly good results for browns, rainbows, and a few hybridized Apache trout, mostly small, while beautiful little upper tributaries like **Castle, Buckalou,** and **Coleman creeks** hold both Arizona natives and Arizona x rainbow hybrids. The head of Coleman flows alongside the Coronado Trail for three miles. Occasionally, Arizona trout up to 10 inches can be pulled out of roadside beaver ponds just a few feet from the roadway. The oddly-colored trout in Buckalou have puzzled some biologists. They could be a Gila-type trout similar to those still found in Spruce Creek in neighboring New Mexico.

Below Luce Ranch, Campbell Blue Creek has in the past been grazed down and degraded, the fishing is slow. Here it makes a short detour into New Mexico to join with **Dry Blue Creek**, then re-enters Arizona a mile below. Federally endangered loach minnows are present in both lower Campbell Blue and the main Blue River. Dry Blue is a New Mexico stream for its entire length. It receives good springs shortly above its join with Campbell Blue Creek, and reproduction of brown trout here is excellent; water quality in recent years has been superior to Campbell Blue Creek where the two meet. In the summer of 1995, Dry Blue held cold, clean water at its mouth with Campbell Blue, which other stream was dry at that particular spot for a period of weeks. Upstream, bi-state tributary **Pace Creek** also has a growing population of browns following a few years of stream improvement by a recently rejuvenated beaver colony and improved watershed conditions, this in turn followed a rest from grazing.

Bush Creek holds rainbow trout in its lower 1/2 mile, most of it on private property. Its population holds in small beaver ponds and is supplemented by escapees from a private fish farm upstream.

Lamphier Canyon and its small but permanent tributary **Indian Creek** drain the north slope of 8500-foot Bear Mountain within the Blue Range Primitive Area. Rainbow trout to 10 inches hide beneath the willows in the lower reaches of the canyon. Smaller fish are scattered above. This stream is hard to fish, but I've had success in the past. Assume a good trout is in every pool, then find a good hiding place and cast upstream. You cannot look for fish in the water without scaring them.

Upper **Grant Creek**, paralleled by a good trail leading from Hannagan Meadow, has its own tiny **unnamed tributary**, plus **Long Cienega**. These upper waters hold Arizona natives of undetermined purity, most quite small. Over-grazing is severe, affecting fishing quality. The lower reach of the stream below Steeple Mesa has no trail through a hard-to-access canyon and has slightly better fishing. I've caught 12-inch Arizona-rainbow hybrids a mile or so above the often-dry mouth of the stream, also an occasional brown of similar size. The main branch has six fishable miles, both

branches combined have maybe one or so.

Foote Creek is similar in nature to Grant and has been even more heavily grazed. It forks about six miles above the Blue, where a small population of what look like rainbow trout survive in four miles of water; it is dry in its lower end. A herd of mountain bighorn sheep, around 80 of them, has been placed here where they reside on steep, redrock bluffs above Foote Creek Canyon. The trail along the upper creek used to resemble a barnyard, now looks like an abandoned barnyard.

The Blue's best tributary is roadless **KP Creek**, flowing through a 3500-foot-deep canyon almost straight below 9400-foot Blue Peak and the aptly-named Sawed-off Mountain. This stream holds Arizona trout of up to 13 inches, stemming from re-introductions in the 1960s, in the foamy pools of its **upper two branches,** each of which provides two to three miles of good habitat, deeply shaded by blue spruce, Douglas fir trees, bracken ferns, and lush streamside vegetation. The branches join together in a twin waterfalls below which are seven or so miles filled with rainbow-AZ hybrids, plus **two more tiny tributaries,** one directly below Blue Lookout Tower, both containing ice-cold spring water and overlooked trout of surprising size. Below the last of these tributaries, the streamside trail climbs out of the canyon and onto KP Mesa. While the upper stream reaches are not often fished, below this point the stream sees extremely few visitors within a narrow box. A mile or two downstream from the lowest trail crossing lies another falls below which the stream is accessible from the Blue River; here the fish look more like rainbows. KP Creek usually flows all the way into the Blue, and on hot summer days rainbows sometimes congregate in the cold water at its mouth.

Seldom-fished **Raspberry, Strayhorse,** and **Thomas creeks** flow into the Blue in its roadless section within the Blue Range Primitive Area. Raspberry and Strayhorse currently hold rainbows in their lower reaches, as well as many suckers and dace; both reportedly are being considered for re-introduction of Gila trout (of the Spruce Creek lineage). Raspberry, steep, wild, and flowing mostly above 6000 feet, is a good coldwater stream, though a bit small, with sufficient rainbow trout in its lower reaches. Its mouth is dry, but trout appear about a half-mile up. Strayhorse also holds rainbows for a mile or two above the Blue River but is slightly lower in elevation and slightly closer to a warmwater habitat. Both these streams flow west to east, exposing them to the sun, which warms the water considerably in the several open reaches that have been heavily grazed by cattle for many decades. With recent grazing curtailments, both of these streams should recover nicely. Strayhorse is accessible by good Forest Service trails (FT 20, FT 31, and FT 89) from US 191 at the head of the stream.

Thomas Creek is the lowest and warmest of all the Blue's trout tributaries and is something of a mystery, at least to me. I have heard reports of trout living here, as well as in tributary **Rosensock**

Green sunfish

Creek, both running off 8300-foot Rose Peak's eastern side below oak and juniper scrub. The elevation of the lower end, where the water is, is roughly 5000 feet. Streams of this character are very marginal, and Thomas is no exception. I visited both streams in 1995 and found only dace in Rosensock. Thomas was dry above the juncture of the two. *¿Que va?* Not to worry, this has happened to me before on other Arizona streams—many times, in fact. When rainfall is sufficient, there could be fair numbers of trout in the lowermost parts of these two creeks, and even in small portions of tributary **Squaw Creek**, as new recruits from the Blue re-enter the stream when the drought conditions subside. So fear not Reader, the hiking trip down to Thomas Creek mouth from the Coronado Trail, then down the Blue to the mouth of warmwater Pigeon Creek, makes a great October or April trip. You'll find trout in the Blue, plus maybe a few elsewhere. My best? 17 inches, between Pigeon and Thomas creek mouths.

In 1995, under pressure from the Arizona Fish and Game Department and various environmental organizations over Apache trout, loach minnow, northern goshawk, and other threatened wildlife populations, the Forest Service ordered cattle reductions of 50 to 80 percent in the Alpine Ranger District, with many of these reductions slated for the upper Blue River watershed. Further cutbacks were made in 1998 as part of a negotiated settlement with a Tucson-based environmental group. If these isolated actions reflect a change in the management of this particular national forest, look for the Blue River and tributaries to start providing fishing quality comparable to that now found on nearby Apache tribal lands, home to the best trout fishing in the Southwest. Even so, as I write, the Blue still has sediment and water temperature problems. My last (auto) inspection tour of the Blue, in August, 1998, showed improvements in the upper part of Campbell Blue (above the Coronado Trail crossing) and no great changes along the lower stream. There were, nonetheless, a number of attractive new signs, most describing a recent re-introduction of the lobo (or "Mexican") wolf. One wolf was shot and killed by a tourist at Blue Crossing Campground in the spring of 1998. Don't let this worry you, however: Most campers here are peaceful and not prone to shoot.

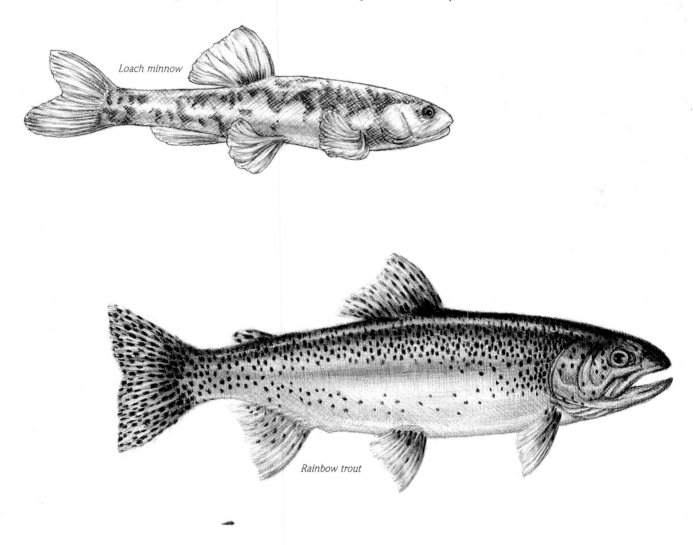

Loach minnow

Rainbow trout

16. EAGLE CREEK SYSTEM

Name: Eagle Creek
Location: East Eagle Creek RARE II Roadless Area, Apache-Sitgreaves National Forest, Apache and Graham Counties, Arizona
Maps: A-S NF Visitors Map, Clifton USGS 1:100,000 series
Elevation: 7000-3200 feet
Length of Fishing Water: 50 miles
Average Flow: Approx. 25 cfs
Best Times: April, May, September-November
Fish Species: Brown trout, rainbow trout, Sonoran sucker, longfin dace, speckled dace, possibly loach minnow, smallmouth bass
Fishable Tributaries: Cottonwood Canyon, Cienega Creek, Willow Creek, Middle Prong, East Eagle Creek, Chitty Canyon, Salthouse Canyon (few trout), Middle Prong, Chitty Canyon, Willow Creek, Cienega Creek, Cottonwood Spring

EAGLE CREEK SYSTEM

Streams along the rim seem to come in matched sets, and the Blue River has its own 50-mile lower-elevation twin, **Eagle Creek**. This marginal stream flows south off the rim, roughly paralleling the Blue while flowing 18 miles west of it. Summer heat here is oppressive, though it's not as bad as at Payson or Camp Verde. Yet, surrounded by grassland mesas in its lower part yielding upstream to ponderosa-topped ridges of 7500-8500 feet to the northwest and northeast, Eagle Creek's middle valley is lower, broader, and hotter than the Blue. Evaporation cools the water in the middle reaches, but not the air. At the stream's lower end is a deep box canyon.

The entire stream used to be well-shaded and cool, supporting a healthy population of native trout, probably the same Gila-type trout which inhabited the neighboring Blue River in equal abundance. The lower end of the stream passes through the San Carlos Apache tribal and Phelps Dodge Mining Corporation lands, then flows through a small BLM-administered National Conservation Area into the Gila River, within the roadless box canyon, west of Clifton, Arizona. It is momentarily diverted in its lower reaches to the mill below the Morenci open pit copper mine. The Phelps Dodge Copper Corporation keeps Eagle Creek running at minimum year-round levels because of the needs for the mill; supplemental water is pumped from wells into the streambed at a number of upstream locations. A major tributary, **Willow Creek**, is also re-charged with water pumped from the Black River on the northern boundary of the San Carlos Reservation, through Big Prairie, then over a low divide. Above the reservation and within the Apache-Sitgreaves National Forest boundary, most of Eagle Creek's stream bottom is private ranch land, some of it bordering the res. Most of the upper creek lies beside a graded Forest Service Road (FR 217) ending at Honeymoon Campground at 5300 feet.

In this vicinity where the stream forks in several directions, with trout continuing upstream into **East Eagle Creek**, the upper tributaries become confined within mountain foothills covered with scrub oak and junipers. Here, as below, the water is gravelly and shaded by scattered old narrowleaf cottonwoods, occasionally with boxelders or Arizona walnut. The headwaters and the middle valley are heavily grazed and water warms considerably in summer below the campground. Arizona G&F stocks the stream at Honeymoon every April, whereupon miners and mill-workers on holiday crowd the area for two or three weeks until most of the "puss-bows" are gone. Some carryover fish survive the year-round, but the precious few wild brown trout which until recently held out in portions of the stream are now said to be gone. They probably checked out during the hot and dry spell of 1994 and 1995. Upstream from here, East Eagle Creek lies within a shaded canyon providing some year round fishing for rainbows to fifteen inches.

Extreme upper tributary **Chitty Canyon** drains straight down the rim, seven miles into East Eagle Creek, and contains "mystery" trout above the 20-foot Chitty Falls. These fish have tentatively been identified as Gila x rainbow, and can be found as far downstream as East Eagle Creek above Dry Prong. Fishing is good within and above a decades-old riparian exclosure above the mouth of **Salt House Canyon**, which also holds occasional stray trout in wet seasons. Above the mouth of Chitty Canyon, trout in East Eagle Creek are very few, although the stream normally flows for several miles above. Tributary Crabtree Creek also has water, but I don't recall ever seeing fish there.

One reason Gila trout, not Apaches, are thought to have been

ARIZONA TROUT: A FLY FISHING GUIDE

native to the entire Eagle Creek system is because of the historical presence of the still-abundant upper Gila River form of the round-tail chubs (*Gila robusta*), which seem always to be a companion species to Gila trout and are thus seen as a sort of marker for the trout's natural occurrence. The spawning chubs in Eagle Creek have peculiar red streaks on the venter and pectoral fins and act very much like game fish, following hatches and hooking themselves on fly fishermen's lures intended for Eagle Creek's much scarcer rainbow and hybrid trout. The chubs thrive in the sun-heated waters, the result of years of watershed abuses, most notably severe overgrazing. East Eagle Creek's steep upper canyon has been repeatedly blown out, almost completely obliterating a former two-rut road up the canyon bottom. A few divots of land are left stranded in the vast gravel beds above Dry Prong mouth, some containing old cottonwood groves growing in a foot or two of soil, some even showing portions of the old road, now hanging several feet above the present creek bottom. The whole watershed has been so heavily impaired for so long that complete recovery of quality trout habitat on Eagle Creek could take several decades. Even so, the complete removal of streamside cattle in 1996 has provided lush new willow growth, and trout are once again reproducing all the way into the box canyon on the creek's lower end. Bass have recently ascended from Willow Creek but they don't seem to do as well. This fisherman is looking for further improvements on East Eagle in the next decade or so.

The still-overgrazed **Middle Prong** watershed of Eagle Creek drains the San Carlos Reservation, heading in low country below the rim, and has for years held very few brown and somewhat more rainbow trout; it can be accessed by a rough spur road dead-ending at the reservation border. Wet Prong isn't.

The stretch of Eagle Creek above the box and below Honeymoon Campground is too warm to fish during summer months. The above-mentioned Willow Creek, plus **Cienega Creek,** drain the reservation's 7500-foot Nantac Mountains, enter-

ing Eagle Creek from the west, farther downstream. These are in steep terrain and both hold roundtail chubs and green sunfish, while Willow Creek holds a virtually unfished population of smallmouth bass. Few people ever enter the deep canyon in the stream's middle reaches. There is the possibility of occasional rainbow trout refugees from the Eagle Creek mainstem entering both of these streams. Water quality is excellent on Willow Creek, with its guaranteed minimum flow and summer water temperatures in the 70s. I've found numbers of what I believe are *Isoperla*, or little yellow stonefly nymphs, on the lower end. These normally signify trout.

Cienega Creek is much smaller than Willow, shrinking down to standing pools in the dry months. At its upper end, remote 2-acre **Maggie Jones Tank,** one of more than 100 on the San Carlos Reservation, may hold a few fish at 5600 feet. Another upper tributary of Willow Creek is dammed to form **Point of Pines Lake,** which always holds rainbow trout. Tiny **Pine Flat Tank,** in another side canyon, is less reliable and much harder to reach at 6000 feet. On the east side of Eagle Creek, the stretch of Cottonwood Canyon just below cold, clean **Cottonwood Springs** occasionally holds rainbows—not all the stocked trout in the Eagle Creek system end up in the frying pan.

Rainbow trout tend to move, and the lower, warmer portion of Eagle Creek can be fished in spring and fall, sometimes with very good results—even discounting the chow line following the yearly Easter stocking, which I don't count as angling. My own bait of choice here is a passable #10 *Isoperla* nymph imitation, a generic golden stone pattern with copper wire ribbing, (inspired by the *Isoperla* I picked out of the mouth of Willow Creek). The trick is to find holes and rapids beside eddies which hide the smaller wandering and occasional big holdover rainbows, then twitch the bait slowly off the bottom nearby, as close as possible to their hiding places. With a little luck, a 14-inch trout will tear out into the pool, retrieve the nymph, and try to return to the shade, all in the blink of an eye.

DÜRTEN KAMPMANN

17. STREAMS OF MOUNT GRAHAM

Name: Grant Creek
Location: Safford Ranger District, Coronado National Forest, Apache Gila Counties, Arizona
Elevation: 10,000-5300 feet
Length: 10 miles
Best Times: May to November
Fish Species: Apache x rainbow trout, Apache trout
Tributaries: Post Creek, Moonshine Creek, Soldier Creek

The Pinaleños are a small range floating in the sky, visible above all others in southeastern Arizona. They rise to 10,770 feet on Mt. Graham and form a crossroads between Mexico's Sierra Madre, the Rocky Mountains, and the Colorado Plateau. They are very small, less than 100,000 acres in size, and completely surrounded by desert. A few blue-colored Durango spruce dot the highest canyons of the northern Sierra Madre. A relict forest of Engelmann spruce rests at the very top. For all practical purposes, the species ends here. A few Engelmann spruce inhabit the crest of the Chiricahuas, a range just to the south and clearly visible, but beyond that the subarctic spruce cannot find a place to live, until two similar types of tree, the sacred fir, appears on the upper slopes of the 15- to 18-thousand-foot peaks of southern Mexico's line of volcanoes, marking the southern boundary of North America. The great mountain here at the top of the Penaleños steals thunder and rain from the surrounding skies, producing a local type of weather all year long. No fewer than twelve trout streams flow down from the range's single dividing ridge, all of them drying up by the time they reach the base of the mountain. The streams all hold introduced populations; there are no records of trout having occurred here in the last century. Most are accessible via the only road to speak of on the entire range, the switchbacking, partly paved Swift Trail (Arizona 366) which climbs to the ridge and almost all the way to the top of the peak. The Gila River passes directly below the range on the northeast, nearly 8000 feet below the crest, but it is a desert stream now and has been for perhaps ten- to twenty-thousand years.

All twelve of the trout streams in this range head in the few thousand acres of spruce-fir timber surrounding the summits of Mt. Graham and Emerald Peak. Two stream systems, those of **Grant Creek** and **Big Canyon Creek**, are on the southwest slope of the range, the other four are on the northeast.

Big Canyon Creek, a beautiful little step-across stream, can be reached from the Swift Trail (AZ 366) at the Hospital Flat picnic grounds. The pure springs which form the stream pour into its sedge-filled bed at well over 9000 feet above the sea. You might well think you are in Banff National Park here. Small Apache trout can be seen right at the bridle path leading away from the various picnic tables. You can follow the stream down for a mile or two, but the farther down you go, the tougher the going gets. You can actually fall off the mountain and get killed trying to climb down and follow the water. The little Apache trout have keen vision, but if you can hide from them they are very easy to catch. A big one from Big Canyon will be 8 inches or so.

Farther along the south face of the mountain, the **Grant Creek** system holds a surprising number of wild Apache trout in upper reaches and what look to me like Apache-rainbow hybrids in the desert below. Excellent fishing can be found on the desert floor, behind a state "country club" prison situated at old Fort Grant at 4700 feet. A rough road ascends the dry bed of Grant Creek for a couple of miles, then dies. The trout can be found by hiking another half mile or so upstream. Here the water seems to come from nowhere, with pools up to seven feet deep under dense cover of live oak on the benches, Gooddings willow thickets, sycamores arching over the streambed, and boxelders wedged into rock crannies. There are a number of good pools and I have caught hybrids to 14 inches here. I bet there are some even larger. The trail (FT 305) along the stream, can be followed from here all the way to the top of the mountain. Don't try ascending tributaries like

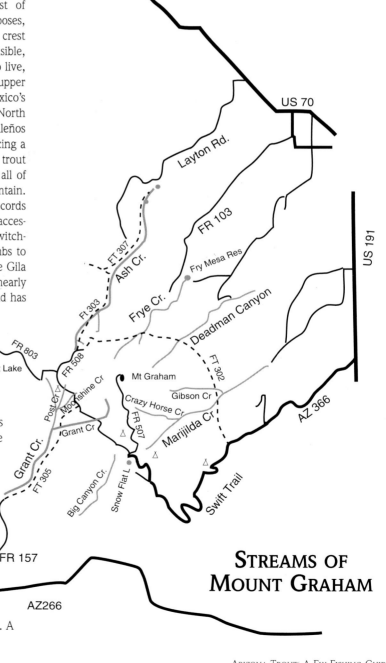

STREAMS OF MOUNT GRAHAM

Moonshine Creek, however. Waterfalls leave this stream hanging far above the green valley where the other streams join. Excellent access to the middle part of Grant Creek, plus sparkling tributaries **Soldier Creek** and **Post Creek**, is available from the same Forest Trail 305 from the top of the mountain, three miles down. You need to stick with this trail because it is just as hard to follow the streambed of Grant Creek down from the mountaintop as it is to follow Big Creek Canyon.

There are a couple of lakes atop the Pinaleños, also: **Snow Flat Lake** (1 acre, 8900 feet) s a bathtub-sized impoundment just under the south side of 10,000-ft Heliograph Peak. A few rainbows are deposited here occasionally. A tiny stream flows out of the bathtub and joins Big Canyon after several waterfalls. All told, the most popular fishing destination on Mount Graham is **Riggs Flat Lake**, filled by snowmelt at 9000 feet and large enough at 11 acres to allow electric motors. Most of the time in summer it is ringed with anglers sitting on lawn chairs, waiting patiently for planted rainbows. They "still-fish" with power bait, cheese, corn, and so forth. There is no reproduction here, but some planted fish survive over the winter and grow larger, up to 18 inches.

One of the streams on the north side of the mountain, **Marijalda Creek**, draining just below Shannon Park and the north side of Heliograph Peak, contains brook char, the rest contain rainbows, hybrids, and Arizona's native Apache trout. There are no records of trout having been originally found here, undoubtedly because of wildfires and killer 250-year droughts. Marijalda has reasonably good fishing in its upper waters in the spruce fir zone, after a five-mile climb via the Round-the-Mountain Trail (FT 302). The lower, desert reaches, straight down, have more rattlesnakes than trout. Farther off the mountain and just south of Safford lies **Roper Lake** (32 acres, 3140 feet), in its namesake state park. There are small warm springs in the park, a captive population of the endangered Gila topminnow in spe-

cially protected pools and, in the impoundment itself, largemouth bass and winter plants of rainbow trout.

In the Marijalda headwaters tributary, **Crazy Horse Creek** has small brookies from time to time. To get there you climb up one and a half miles above the Round-the-Mountain Trail Crossing. Lower tributary **Gibson Creek**, one ridge over from Marijalda, is also very marginal and extremely hard to fish. You'll do more climbing than fishing, at least from the Round-the-Mountain Trail (FT 302). **Deadman Canyon**, which threads its way below a nasty-looking pinnacle called Deadman Peak before drying out and draining down to the Gila River, is only slightly more promising than Gibson but a good deal easier to follow. The Douglas fir shade and alder thickets along the canyon bottom stand out in stark contrast to the sun-blasted juniper scrubland on the slopes above. Roadless **Frye Creek** and its forks have better flow, deeper water, wild trout and an old sawmill site to boot. These provide water for 4-acre, 6500-foot **Frye Mesa Reservoir**, a water source for Thatcher, Arizona, stocked with rainbows and barely reachable from that small town by a steep, rough road (FR 103).

The **Ash Creek system** provides the best overall habitat for trout on the north side of the mountain, easily reachable by trail (FT 302 and FT 303) via spur road FR 508. These descend from the top of the mountain at Emerald Camp. FT 307 ascends from below the mountain at the old Cluff Ranch (now a state nature preserve), whose two

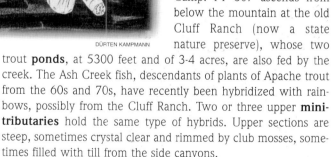

DÜRTEN KAMPMANN

trout **ponds**, at 5300 feet and of 3-4 acres, are also fed by the creek. The Ash Creek fish, descendants of plants of Apache trout from the 60s and 70s, have recently been hybridized with rainbows, possibly from the Cluff Ranch. Two or three upper **mini-tributaries** hold the same type of hybrids. Upper sections are steep, sometimes crystal clear and rimmed by club mosses, sometimes filled with till from the side canyons.

18. CHIRICAHUA MOUNTAINS

Name: Cave Creek
Location: Chiricahua Wilderness, Coronado National Forest
Maps: Coronado NF Visitors Map, Douglas RD, USGS 1:100,000 series, Chiricahua Peak edition
Elevation: 7000-5000 feet
Length of Fishing Water: 6 miles
Best Times: April, May, September-November
Fish Species: longfin dace, speckled dace (possible re-introduction site for Gila trout)
Tributaries: South Fork Cave Creek, Cima Creek, upper branch

As you look at the small, isolated mountain ranges always within view in southern Arizona, it is easy to guess which ones today have permanent waters. To gather sufficient rainfall for even one tiny stream, a small range requires at least one peak or ridge of close to 9000 feet. The Santa Rita and Huachuca mountains of southeastern Arizona have such peaks, while the Baboquivari and Rincon Ranges do not.

Streams capable of supporting trout populations require something more, however. The uplifted mass must be large enough to provide for several peaks of 8500 to 9000 feet or higher. The Santa Catalina Mountains have an elongated ridge of such height and

careful inspection reveals one deep canyon and one small stream system which does indeed provide some trout habitat. Mount Graham, by contrast, is part of the slightly smaller but much higher Pinaleño Range; at nearly 10,800 feet it's the highest point among the desert ranges of southern Arizona and higher than all but one or two of the mountains of neighboring Sonora and Chihuahua. This small range provides a cluster of tiny streams where wild trout have been successfully introduced.

Largest and wildest of all of southeastern Arizona's "Sky Islands" is the 300,000-acre Chiricahua Range, which has also shown itself capable of supporting wild-trout populations for decades. This range is also set apart from the others in that it is actually the northern terminus of the 1000-mile-long Sierra Madre Occidental, the formidable and nearly impassable backbone of northwestern Mexico. The animals and plants of the Chiricahuas seem more Mexican than American—Apache and Chihuahua pines, streamside cypress trees, coati-mundi and ringtail cats, all as common here as anywhere in the *barranca* country farther south, below the *frontera*. The crest of the Chiricahuas is actually a Madrean divide; the streams of the southern half of the range drain into the Rio Bavispe system of Sonora and Chihuahua, emptying into the Sea of Cortez near Los Mochis.

None of the mountains of southern Arizona have ever been known to contain endemic trout populations, however. All trout contained in the few streams have arisen from plantings dating back anywhere from fifteen to ninety years. I remember being told years ago that "native" trout still persisted in the Chiricahuas below Anita Spring. What the term "native" meant in this case is hard to tell. There is no record of any original populations of trout in any of the Chiricahua watersheds, while today's streams all dry up long before they begin their journey to their downstream recipient drainages. Each separate stream system is completely isolated from the rest. That was not the case 100 years ago, but it is today.

The reason trout were originally unreported in these mountains can be vividly illustrated by a fire that spread through the Chiricahuas in the summer of 1994. In May of that year this 9974-foot range thirty miles north of the Mexican border contained nine live trout streams, including a couple of my favorite streams anywhere. A lightening-caused forest fire in June, however, dubbed the Rattlesnake Fire, burned the crowns of the pine and Douglas fir timber along the entire main ridge, and subsequent summer rains sent many tons of muck down each stream. In October 1994, after having been told that all the trout in the entire range had died, I inspected six streams and found only a very few rainbow trout surviving in one stream in the range's southern end, **Rucker Canyon**, just below its tiny impoundment, 10-acre **Rucker Lake**. The little pond had been filled to the brim with mud batter; under the hot October sun it bubbled like one of the paint pot hot springs in Yellowstone Park.

Native warmwater minnow species like the longfin dace and Mexican stoneroller in downstream reaches of this stream and neighboring Leslie Canyon were doing quite well, in contrast to the exotic introduced trout. These trout had been decimated in the headwaters of Rucker and apparently exterminated from all of the other streams. In particular, the fate of the brook char population in upper Rucker Canyon was sealed. This former southernmost brook char population in the United States is now gone.

Thus, the trout are now gone from at least four and perhaps up to eight streams, where any re-appearance of trout will have to come by the *deus ex machina* of the game department. Even fine little streams like **Cave Creek** and **South Fork Cave Creek** will have to receive such help. Clearly, if such a fire had occurred in 1794, 1294, 594 AD, or earlier, trout could not have returned, for even though perhaps two or more of the range's streams might have flowed through to the Sea of Cortez in the recent geologic past, only warmwater species would have had chance to find passage through the San Simon, Sulfur Springs, or San Bernadino valleys below the Chiricahuas. Furthermore, it would seem highly likely that one or more fires similar in nature to the 1994 blaze would have actually occurred over the last ten- to twenty-thousand years, or more precisely since the last time trout might have been able to live in the middle Gila and Bavispe rivers. Certainly such fires are possible, and over sufficient length of time possibility equals likelihood. All this explains precisely why none of the smaller and more isolated mountain ranges in the American Southwest and in Sonora and Chihuahua, Mexico contain endemic trout populations.

On the other hand, larger, more complex ranges, such as the northern Mexico cordillera, the Mogollon Mountains of New Mexico and Arizona's White Mountains, could not possibly have seen all their streams ruined by any fire or series of fires. There always remained unaffected streams providing temporary refuge for trout populations, while large coldwater refuges such as the Black and White rivers remained in constant communication with nearly all streams, providing eventual means for re-colonization of lost populations. Thus, each stream which lost its trout could eventually regain them. As a result, the major ranges could hold trout in natural equilibrium with periodic destructive fires, while the smaller ranges could not. Such considerations also underscore, once again, how remarkable it is that native trout have been able to survive as long as they have in the semi-arid and desert Southwest.

The best natural trout habitat in the Chiricahuas is the Cave Creek system which has four, maybe five branches capable of supporting trout. The stream has carved a hidden canyon within a natural fold in the main ridge of the range. The beautiful little section below Cathedral Rock and Portal Peak has been called "Arizona's Yosemite," to compare great things to small. I have caught very nice browns to 15 inches here, all descendants of an original stocking in the 1930s, plus rainbow trout equally large, these latter in a multitude of forms and colors— all wild, stream-born fish. I have even caught brook char in the system. Where or when this species was planted I have no idea,

Crayfish

other than that it was long ago. The best water has always been the main branch above Herb Martyr Campground all the way to Chiricahua Falls, and the entire upper South Fork, both off-limits to livestock. The South Fork below the aptly-named Maple Canyon is a noted destination for birders who are able to add a number of Madrean species to their American life lists, basically because of the South Fork's healthy riparian vegetation, something not found in very many permanent or even seasonal streams in the range. In most of the other parts of the Chiricahuas where cattle congregate, for instance in two other small tributaries entering Cave Creek from the north, there are generally few birds and even fewer fish.

The Rattlesnake Fire has now wiped the slate clean in the Chiricahuas, and there are at present only the vaguest of plans to restock any of the waters with trout. If stocking does occur at a later date, expect Gila-type trout to be placed in the Cave Creek, East and West Turkey and perhaps Rock Creek drainages. Rucker Canyon, which still holds a few rainbows, lies across the Madrean divide, draining into the Rio Yaqui. This river system holds one or more native trout species/subspecies of its own (undescribed by formal science at this late date).

Herb Martyr and **John Hands lakes** are the names of two former trout impoundments, each a couple of acres in size, where rainbow trout were planted in the 1960s and early 70s. Each has filled in entirely with rubble and sediment, creating a waterfalls at each former damsite, plus plunge pools directly below. Exactly the same thing happened to **Rucker Lake** at the southern end of the range in 1994. These expensive, artificial waterfalls show the relative un-wisdom of building impoundments in canyon areas in rugged desert mountains. The **South Fork** has (i.e. had) its best fishing, especially in good rainfall years, one to four miles above the graded dead-end access road, FR 42C, all the way by trail (FT 243) to an upper falls. Its lower mile or so is normally dry in summer. The main stream formerly had an amazing number of fish along the entirety of the paved road passing the old ranger station, down to a diversion into an irrigation ditch just below the station. **Cima Creek** is very, very small, but I have caught browns to 13 inches there. Even in wet years, you might have to walk a half mile or so just to find one pool capable of supporting a few fish.

In spite of the throngs of birders and other tourists and the crowded campgrounds along lower Cave Creek, I have never seen another fisherman along it, or along any Chiricahua stream for that matter. I have caught beautiful trout from April through October right within the Cave Creek Forest Service campgrounds. During low water the fish seek refuge under large boulders and undercut banks, feeding only in low light. Sometimes the flow is interrupted by dry, bleached gravel beds, but the water always remains cold enough to keep trout active.

East Turkey Creek, flowing eastwards, just north of the Cave Creek system, has always held many longfin dace and very, very few (rainbow) trout, none of which I have ever been able to find. The trout are now gone from this stream, also.

West Turkey Creek, plus tributary **Ward Canyon** on the other side of the range, flows west into the Sulphur Springs valley and might still contain small rainbow trout. **Rock Creek,** slightly to the north, has held a few more in the past. At this time no one knows what's there.

Rucker Canyon, previously mentioned, once held small, easily-caught brook char above Rucker Lake and rainbows below, the latter escapees from regular plantings at the lake. Today the rainbows are barely surviving below the dam.

There is also a secret pond at the head of **Horseshoe Canyon**, on the East side of the Chiricahuas, formerly said to hold pan-sized rainbow trout. I have never verified these reports.

I have spent many a delightful afternoon in the Chiricahuas, far up into the mountaintops, stalking and catching wild trout. When the fish were there, in the streams, no one else seemed to know anything about them. Now they are gone from nearly the whole mountain range and I find myself describing a temporal mirage. Perhaps what happened here is a foresight of what lies ahead in the Southwest and elsewhere. Maybe, one day, fly fishing for wild trout will itself be an anachronism, as all that is wild and natural disappears from sight and memory. Fortunately, by then this fisherman will be long gone; and by then, perhaps, enjoying oneself as much as I have here will have long since been declared illegal.

19. SANTA CATALINA MOUNTAINS

Name: Sabino Canyon
Location: Pusch Ridge Wilderness, Santa Catalina Mountains north of Tucson
Maps: Coronado National forest Visitors Map, Santa Catalina District; USGS 1:100,000 series, Tucson edition
Elevation: 8000-3000 feet
Length of fishing water: 8 miles
Best Times: April, May, September- November
Fish Species: Brown trout, longfin dace,
Tributaries: Lemmon Canyon

The Santa Catalina Mountains, a high-elevation 9500-ft range rising out of the Sonoran Desert, looming over and now half-surrounded by the city of Tucson, lie far to the south of the Mogollon Rim. Yet they are still, on rare clear days, visible from its eastern edge, and from the Blue Range near the New Mexico line. Like the Chiricahuas and Mount Graham, the Catalinas are one of Arizona's basin-and-range "Sky islands;" unlike the others, this range holds exotic *palo verde* ("green stick") thickets and saguaros in its lower slopes. It never contained trout, but it does get 30 inches of yearly precipitation at the crest, and holds four or five small permanent streams; trout have been planted into three of these. The plantings of brown trout into south-draining **Sabino** and its tributary **Lemmon Canyon** were most successful, forming wild populations which still exist in 5 to 8 miles of permanent waters within the Pusch Ridge Wilderness Area. More uncertain results have come from the rainbows planted occasionally into neighboring **Romero Canyon**, a stream on the west edge of the Santa Catalinas, with interrupted and extremely small summer flow. **Rose Canyon Lake**, 7 acres at 7000 feet, is just off the

Hitchcock Highway, a tourist drive zigging up to the summit, and about two-thirds the way to the top of the range. Sitting just below 8500-ft. Mt. Bigelow, this campground reservoir is heavily stocked with rainbows from May to September, and even more heavily fished. You won't find such crowds if you decide to fish for the wild browns in Sabino; although the lower stream does have a side trail accessing its inner canyon up as far as the mouth of the creek's dry west fork, not many fishermen climb into the steep upper end to have a look. The mouth of the canyon, spilling into the de-watered Riito Creek in suburban Tucson, looks good but is fishless. No easy way to get at the browns in this stream, or in Lemmon Creek, either. That's why they're still there.

20. CHUSKA MOUNTAINS

Name:	Tsaile Creek
Location:	Navaho Indian Reservation, Apache County
Elevation:	8200-6300 feet
Length of Fishing Water:	14 miles
Best Times:	April, May, September-November
Fish Species:	rainbow trout
Tributaries:	unnamed

The 9800-foot, fir, aspen, and pine-covered Chuska Mountains, running roughly north-south for about 70 miles, and the 7000-foot Defiance Plateau, covered with pine and juniper, spreading beyond the southern end of the range, lie in both extreme northeastern Arizona and adjoining New Mexico. These flat-topped mountain lands were once the home of the Annasazi Indians, who continuously inhabited Canyon de Chelley and Canyon del Muerto for over 2000 years. The Chuskas are not a major range, by any means. From the top, you can see desert on

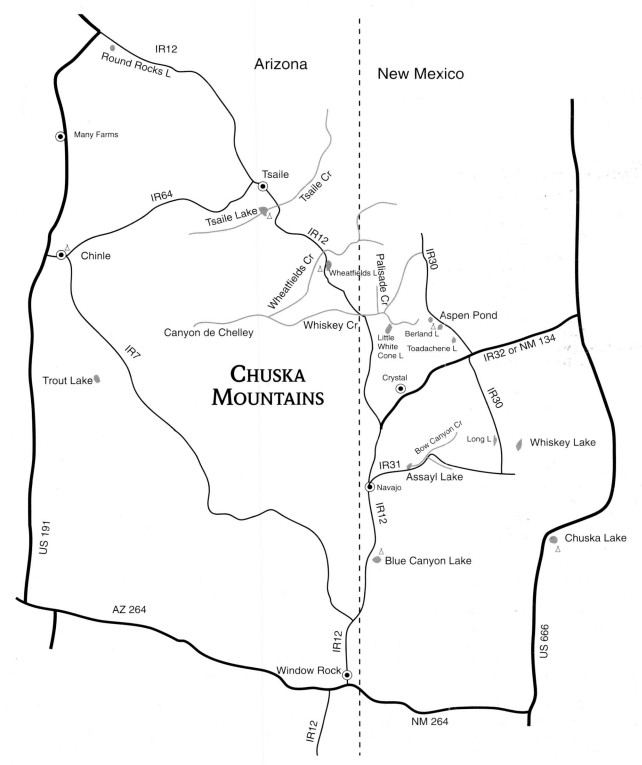

both sides, beneath broken mesas that almost seem alive, trailing away in the foreground. The Navajo sandstone that sweeps around the pillars and buttes of these mountains is sunset red, and so is the coat of dust. The summit snowpack in the western San Juan Mountains in nearby Colorado is sometimes painted a faint orange in May, by Navajo sandstorms. Yet the west slope of the Chuskas, which looms over the two major canyons, provided water and timber for the villages that lined their course for many forgotten centuries of human life. Accelerated erosion and ecological changes occurred during this period, and the pueblos were abandoned in the 1300s, possibly due to flood, drought, timber shortages, or something else not yet thought of by today's archaeologists. Theories for the disappearance abound, including even cannibalism. The Canyon de Chelley was rediscovered, ironically, by the inimical Navajos in the early 1700s, who used it as a fortress stronghold against the Spanish, Kit Carson, and others. The entire area is today within the 16 million acres of the Navajo Indian Reservation, and the Navajos, whose cattle and sheep wander over the ruins, seem bemused by the civilization of their ancient predecessors.

A number of streams in the Chuska and connecting Lukachukai mountains apparently once held a population of Colorado cutthroat trout, which is fitting since this range more properly belongs with the Ute and San Juan mountains. A strongly-colored specimen of the Colorado cutthroat subspecies, hybridized with the rainbow trout, was reported from the Chuskas in 1979, from a collection in 1974.

The eastern edge of the range is steep. Most of the water flows westward into Arizona, and into the Chinle Wash, of which del Muerto and de Chelley are the principal tributaries, and from there into the San Juan River. The Canyon de Chelley region has suffered from assorted forms of modern-day ecological stress over recent decades, of an order or two greater than in the earlier days, and the trout streams of the Chinle drainages, now containing naturalized rainbow trout populations, show it. Some are on the verge of disappearing.

Although the lower reaches of Canyon de Chelley and Canyon del Muerto are contained within Canyon de Chelley National Monument, management here is concerned mainly with archaeology and tribal relations, not wildlife or its habitat. This is no Yellowstone. The Park Service could easily prepare an exhibit on desertification within the monument itself. Meanwhile, bulldozers have been at work elsewhere on the reservation, scooping out ponds and reservoirs along the beds of ancient washes. To encourage tourism, the Navaho tribe has filled them with a variety of fish, most notably rainbow trout, but also bullheads, channel catfish, bass, sunfish, and even Nile perch. Emphasis is on the rainbows. Many of these come from the White Mountain Apache hatchery on Williams Creek, but 20- to 30,000 trout are also raised each year at a facility first built in the 1980s on the eastern, dry side of the Chuskas—flow from the spring is a mere 20 gallons per minute.

It is a long drive to the Navajo from the Southwest's population centers. Few non-Navajos fish the lakes, which often provide better fishing than their counterparts in central and eastern Arizona. No state license is required, but a tribal permit is. If you are going to fish the Chuskas, you can pick up your license in Window Rock, Arizona at the foot of the mountains on state highway 264.

TSAILE AND WHISKEY CREEKS

Tsaile Creek flows for 14 miles through the forest, then fills the upper end of Canyon del Muerto. It held Colorado cutthroats in the Annasazi times, supports stream-born rainbow and brown trout today, as does one **small upstream tributary.** Companion **Tsaile Lake** (260 acres, 7050 feet), scooped out of a meadow just inside the Canyon de Chelley National Monument boundary, holds stocked rainbows, channel catfish, exotic cutthroats, and a campground. Within the monument, Tsaile Creek finds the deep Canyon del Muerto, unvisited by fishermen but well-trampled by sheep and cattle.

Wheatfields Creek flows into Canyon de Chelley and is an almost exact counterpart to Tsaile Creek. The creek holds about 11 miles of water, and it too has a companion reservoir, muddy, cow-rimmed **Wheatfields Lake** (270 acres, 7300 feet). Like Tsaile Lake, it too holds wild and stocked rainbows, plus brook char and cutthroat trout. The cutthroats are not the native Colorado variety. An informal campground sits right by the dam, upon which paved Tribal 12 crosses the drainage. Upstream tributaries **Crystal, Whiskey, Palisade,** and **Little Whiskey creeks** also hold rainbows and possibly a few wild browns. Downstream, brutally grazed Canyon de Chelley presents a marginal trout fishing expedition where you can expect more quicksand than fish.

Trout Lake, 26 acres, surrounded by sagebrush at 8900 feet, gets a rainbow stocking each spring. Few anglers find their way here off Tribal Road 7 southeast of Chinle. Electric motors only.

Far out away from the trees, in the Lukachukai drainage, **Round Rock Lake** (50 acres, 5600 feet) is just off US 191, sixteen miles north of Many Farms. The lake is stocked with rainbows and channel catfish, and the rainbows, in particular, grow big in the murky water. Electric motors only, no facilities.

Antelope Lake is shallow, murky, weedy in summer, very small (3 acres), and stocked with rainbows, some of which grow to very respectable size. It lies at 5300 feet a few miles south and west of Window Rock, with a turnoff on AZ 264. Electric motors only.

NAVAJO WATERS IN NEW MEXICO

Two seldom-visited trout streams—plus a number of trout lakes, some of them quite small, but nearly all uncrowded, lie enirely in New Mexico and within the Navajo Reservation. The many small lakes lie on a large, roof-like 9000-foot mesa just east of the state line, filled with spruce, fir, pine, and aspen. The trout streams of the Chuskas all form here, draining to the west. New Mexicans ignore this part of the state. Fishing here is no problem for Arizonans, however, for the tribal license is good in both states. As with their counterparts across the state line, fishing is best in these New Mexico lakes in late spring, when the cottonwoods bud, and in early fall when the aspens first start to turn. All lie between 8700 and 9000 feet above sea level.

Aspen Pond, 7000 feet in elevation and 1 acre in size, holds rainbows. It is just north of Crystal, New Mexico, off Navajo 12. Electric motors only, no facilities.

Berland Lake, 3 acres and 8800 feet, is next to Aspen Pond. A few picnic tables are here along the shore, as well as good numbers of rainbow trout in the water. Primitive camping, electric motors only.

Assayi Lake, 36 acres, 8900 ft., is eleven miles east of Navajo, NM, up in the pines, and holds a few cutthroat trout as well as the usual rainbows. The view to the southwest is a greener, more forested version of Monument Valley.

Just north of Asayi Lake, **Whiskey Lake** is 250 acres and very shallow. Rainbow trout grow fast here in spring, if they survive the winter freeze.

Blue Canyon Lake is 60 acres in size and at 75 feet is the deepest lake on the reservation. Rainbow trout are here, at 8800 feet, as is a primitive camping area. No electric motors.

Toadachene Lake, at 20 acres, is near the Washington Pass Road, and is subject to winterkill. Rainbows are here at 8700 feet.

Long Lake, 50 acres at 8700 feet, is nearby. A few small ponds near **Old Pine Spring** are sometimes stocked.

Chuska Lake, the easternmost trout lake on the Navajo Reservation, is north of Gallup off US 666. This is 25 acres of water in the high desert at 6900 feet. Regularly fished from Gallup, the lake yields rainbows from 10 to 18 inches. Primitive camping and electric motors only.

Bowl Canyon and **Oak Creek** run together as they drain southwestwards through Assayi Lake and on towards a muddy catfish destination called Red Lake, which straddles the Arizona-New Mexico line, and where some rainbow wanderers and a few wild browns have survived in these two streams in the recent past, and may yet. Below the dam and immediately above the lake, in Bowl Canyon, you can find salmon egg jars and old tennis shoes, always a sign of fish.

MISCELLANEOUS WATERS

The Bill Williams River drains from the Bill Williams and Hualapai Mountains north of Prescott and west of Flagstaff, then flows westward to the Colorado River. There are no trout streams here; there are a number of rainbow trout impoundments with no natural reproduction but regular stockings by the state game and fish. I will list these by name only. Most are near Williams, Arizona and easily found: **Dogtown Reservoir,** 3 acres, 7070 feet; **Cataract Lake**, 35 acres, 6800 ft; **Kaibab Lake,** 45 acres, 6790 feet; **Santa Fe Lake**, 3 acres, 6940 feet; and; **Perkins Tank**, 2 acres, 6820 feet.

Elsewhere, in the oak scrub of the mountain foothills of extreme southern Arizona, lie **Sonoita, Parker Canyon, and Peña Blanca lakes** (150, 90 and 50 acres; 3800, 5200 and 3900 feet, respectively), the latter two in the Coronado National Forest. These give relief to water-starved locals and are fished very heavily all year round. All three are stocked with rainbow trout in winter. Yet, with possible exception of 5200-foot Parker Canyon, summers are too warm for the trout to survive in these lakes, and so attention turns to the bass in summer months. Not far away, **Madera, Sycamore, Miller and Ramsey canyons** hold beautiful small streams, Ramsey and Miller of the isolated, 9500-foot Huachuca Mountains right near the Arizona-Sonora border west of Bisbee; Madera in the 9500-foot Santa Rita range; and Sycamore in a research natural area in the lower-elevation Tumacori Mountains, also on the Sonora border.

All four canyons hold live water, although precious little of it, and provide nesting habitat for rare Mexican endemic wildlife, including elegant trogans and other birds of the Sierra Madre. The long-tailed, raccoon-like coati-mundi is highly intelligent and has in some places learned to climb trees and pounce on picnic tables in order to scatter tourists and devour their abandoned fried chicken. These mammals are abundant in the southern ranges, some wandering northwards up to the Mogollon Rim near the New Mexico state line. Sycamore Canyon lies at the head of Mexico's Rio Concepcion, the others near the source of the now-dry but once northflowing Santa Cruz River.

Though its watershed lies almost entirely within Coronado National Forest, a physician once owned much of the private land along upper Ramsey Canyon, largely old mining and homestead patents patiently acquired over many years. For his own enjoyment the good doctor stocked a few pools in the canyon with rainbow trout, particularly the big pool now called Ramsey Pond, in front of his cabin retreat. He lived many years and immediately after his death locals were said to have snuck into the canyon, found the pools, and, apparently, caught all the rainbows, where none remain to this day. The land was willed to the Nature Conservancy and made into a preserve, where trogans coati-mundis, and the rare Tarahumara frog survive. In all likelihood, trout never historically inhabited either Ramsey Canyon or any other streams in these small southern ranges (see Chiricahua Mountains, page 64).

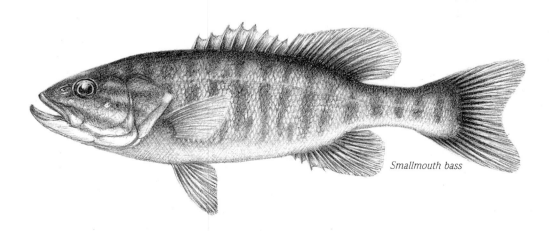

Smallmouth bass

In the following listings, stream tributaries are indented. For example, in the Grand Canyon system below (see highlighted text): Bright Angel Creek is a tributary of the Colorado River, and Roaring Springs is a tributary of Bright Angel Creek.

The Grand Canyon
Colorado River
- North Canyon Creek (trib. to Colorado River)
- Nankoweap Creek
- Unkar Creek
- Vishnu Creek
- Deer Creek
- Bright Angel Creek
  - Roaring Springs
    - Phantom Creek
- Hermit Creek
- Monument Creek
- Pipe Creek
  - Garden Canyon
- Crystal Creek
  - Dragon Creek
- Shinumo Creek
- White Creek
- Tapeats Creek
  - Thunder River
- Deer Creek
- Kanab Creek
- Havasu Canyon
- Diamond Creek

Agua Fria River System
Sycamore Creek

West Verde River System
Verde River (trout rare)
- Sycamore Canyon (trout rare)
- Oak Creek
  - West Fork of Oak Creek
- Wet Beaver Creek
  - Dry Beaver Creek (trout rare)
- West Clear Creek
  - Clover Creek
- Gap Creek (trout extremely rare)
- Fossil Creek (bass)

East Verde Drainage
East Verde River
- Pine Creek
- Webber Creek
  - Bray Creek
- Sycamore Creek
- Chase Creek
- Dude Creek
- Bonita Creek
- Perley Creek
- Ellison Creek
  - small side tributary

East Clear Creek System
East Clear Creek
- General Springs Canyon
- Bear Canyon
- Barbershop Canyon
  - Merritt Draw Canyon
  - Dane Canyon
- Yeager Canyon (very few trout)
- Leonard Canyon
  - Buck Springs Canyon
  - East Fork Leonard Canyon
  - West Fork Leonard Canyon
- Willow Creek (few trout)
  - Gentry Canyon (few trout)
    - Open Draw (few trout)
    - Turkey Creek (few trout)
    - Beaver Creek (few trout)
  - Bear Canyon (few trout)

Chevelon Canyon Drainage
Chevelon Canyon
- West Fork Fork Chevelon (few trout)
- Willow Springs Canyon
- Woods Canyon
- Wildcat Canyon (very few trout)
- Black Canyon (very few if any trout)

Tonto Creek System
Tonto Creek
- Houston Creek
- Haigler Creek
  - Marsh Creek
  - Gordon Canyon Creek
- Christopher Creek
  - Hunter Creek
    - Sharp Creek
- Horton Creek
- Big Canyon
- Dick Williams Creek

Sierra Anchas
Salome Creek
- Workman Creek
  - Rose Creek (very few trout)
  - Reynolds Creek (few trout)
  - McFadden Creek (very few trout)

Cherry Creek
- Pueblo Canyon Creek (very few trout)
- PB Creek (very few trout)

Canyon, Cibecue, Carrizo Creeks
Canyon Creek
- Mule Creek
- Swamp Creek
- Rotten Spring Creek

Cibecue Creek
- White Spring
- CT Spring

Carrizo Creek
- Limestone Canyon

- Corduroy Creek
  - Forestdale Creek
  - Hop Canyon

White River System
White River
- North Fork White River
  - Diamond Creek
    - Coon Creek
    - Little Diamond Creek
      - Cienega Creek
      - unnamed trib.
      - Coyote Creek*
      - Maverick Cienega drainage*
      - unnamed trib.*
    - Sun Creek*
      - tributary*
    - Moon Creek*
      - tributary*
    - Star Creek*
    - North Fork Diamond Creek*
      - headwater tributary*
  - Bull Cienega Creek
  - Gooseberry Creek
    - Gomez Creek
  - Trout Creek
    - Earl Creek*
      - Porcupine Creek
  - Williams Creek
  - Sand Creek
    - Lame Deer Canyon
  - Bog Creek
    - Little Bog Creek
    - Soldier Creek
    - Horseshoe Creek
    - Bar H Creek
  - No Name Creek
  - Paradise Creek
    - Snow Stake Creek
    - Wohlenberg Draw
  - Bear Cienega and Creek
  - Sheep Cienega
  - Ord Creek*
  - Smith Creek*
  - Snake Creek
    - Becker Creek
    - Sunrise Creek
- East Fork White River
  - Firebox Creek
  - Rock Creek
    - tributary
    - tributary
    - tributary
  - Deep Creek*
    - tributary*
  - Elk Canyon*
    - tributary*
  - upper tributary*
  - upper tributary*
  - upper tributary*

Bonito Creek System
Bonito Creek
- Corn Creek
- Tonto Creek
  - Cienega Creek
  - Bull Creek
  - Odart Cienega
- Little Bonito Creek
  - unnamed tributary
  - Crooked Creek
    - Lofer Cienega Creek
      - Boggy Creek
  - unnamed tributary
  - unnamed tributary
- unnamed tributary
- Flash Creek
- unnamed tributary
- Long Canyon
- Squaw Creek
  - unnamed tributary
- Butterfly Creek
- Hurricane Creek
- Hughey Creek
- Duke Creek
- Peasoup Creek

Black River Drainage
Black River
- Turkey Creek
- Paddy Creek
- Ess Creek
  - unnamed tributary
- Pacheta Creek
  - Bluff Cienega
  - headwater tributary
  - headwater tributary
- Bearwallow Creek
  - North Fork Bearwallow Creek
  - South Fork Bearwallow Creek
- Reservation Creek
  - lower unnamed tributary
  - upper unnamed tributary
  - Deep Cienega
  - Soldier Creek
- Snake Creek
- Conklin Creek
  - unnamed tributary
- Fish Creek
  - Double Cienega Creek
    - unnamed tributary
  - Corduroy Creek
- Bear Creek
- Beaver Creek
  - Johns Canyon
  - Horton Creek
  - Willow Creek
  - Thomas Creek
  - Hannagan Creek
  - Hawksnest Canyon
- Centerfire Creek
  - Wildcat Creek Centerfire
  - Boggy Creek

- East Draw
- Blow Draw
West Fork Black River
- headwater tributary
- Thompson Creek
- Burro Creek
- Stinky Creek
- Hayground Creek
- Home Creek
- Horse Creek
East Fork Black River
- North Fork of East Fork
  - Merritt Draw
  - Spence Spring
- Three Rivers Creek
  - unnamed tributary
- Boneyard Creek
- unnamed spring
- Coyote Creek
- Open Draw
- Deer Creek

Little Colorado River System
Little Colorado River
- Concho Creek
  - Mineral Creek*
- Silver Creek
  - Show Low Creek
    - Walnut Creek
      - Porter Creek (very few trout)
  - Carnero Creek (very few trout)
- Coyote Creek (occasional trout)
  - Morrison Creek
  - Mamie Creek
- Nutrioso Creek
  - Rudd Creek
    - Benton Creek
  - Riggs Creek
  - Colter Creek
  - Auger Creek
  - Hulsey Creek (few trout)
  - Paddy Creek
- Water Canyon
- South Fork Little Colorado River
- Fish Creek (very few trout)
- Hall Creek
- Benny Creek
  - Rosie Creek
- Bunch Res. flowage
- West Fork
  - headwater tributary
- East Fork Little Colorado River
  - Lee Valley Creek

San Francisco River System
San Francisco River
- Turkey Creek
- Stone Creek (very few trout)
- Romero Creek (few trout)

Blue River System
Blue River
- Thomas Creek (very few trout)

- Rosensock Creek (very few trout)
- Strayhorse Creek
- Raspberry Creek
- McKittrick Creek (few trout)
- KP Creek
  - headwater tributary
  - middle unnamed tributary
  - unnamed tributary, Blue Lookout
- Grant Creek
  - upper tributary
  - Long Cienega (very few fish)
- Lamphier Canyon
  - Indian Creek (very few fish)
- Foote Creek
  - Right Fork
- Bush Creek
- Dry Blue Creek
  - Pace Creek
- Campbell Blue Creek
  - Castle Creek
    - Buckalou Creek
  - Coleman Creek
  - Cienega Creek (very few trout)

Eagle Creek Drainage
Eagle Creek/East Eagle Creek
- Cottonwood Canyon
- Cienega Creek (very few trout)
- Willow Creek (very few trout)
- Middle Prong (few trout)
- Chitty Canyon
- Salthouse Canyon (occasional trout)

Streams of Mt. Graham
Grant Creek
- Post Creek
- Moonshine Creek
- Soldier Creek
- Big Canyon
- Marijalda Creek
  - Crazy Horse Creek (Marijalda)
  - Gibson Creek (Marijalda)
- Deadman Canyon
- Frye Creek
  - upper tributary
- Ash Creek
  - upper tributary
  - upper tributary

Chiricahua Mountains
Cave Creek (currently no trout)
- South Fork Cave Creek (currently no trout)
  - Cima Creek (currently no trout, little habitat)
- East Turkey Creek (currently no trout, very little habitat)
- West Turkey Creek (currently no trout)
  - Ward Canyon Creek (currently no trout)
- Rock Creek (currently no trout, little habitat)
- Rucker Canyon (currently few trout)

Santa Catalina Mountains
Sabino Canyon

Lemmon Canyon (Sabino)
Romero Canyon

Chuska Mountains
Tsaile Creek
    small tributary
Wheatfields Creek

Whiskey Creek
    Little Whiskey Creek
    Crystal Creek
    Palisade Creek
    small tributary
Bowl Canyon
    Oak Creek

Miscellaneous Waters
Madera Canyon (no trout)
Ramsey Canyon (no trout)
Sycamore Canyon (no trout)

*Closed to fishing to help restore wild populations of Apache trout.

TROUT LAKE LIST

Grand Canyon
    Russell Tank, 1 acre, 7000 ft.

Agua Fria System
    Lynx Lake, 55 acres, 5530 ft.
    Horsethief Lake, 50 acres, 6150 ft.

Verde River System
    Whitehorse Lake, 30 acres, 7000 ft
    JD Dam, 6 acres, 6460 ft

East Verde Drainage
    None

East Clear Creek System
    Blue Ridge Reservoir, 70 acres, 6720 ft.
    Knoll Lake, 55 acres, 7340 ft.
    Bear Canyon Lake, 65 acres, 7560 ft.
    Clear Creek Reservoir, 60 acres, 5000 ft.

Chevelon Canyon Drainage
    Chevelon Canyon Lake, 175 acres, 6380 ft.
    Woods Canyon Lake, 52 acres, 7510 ft.
    Willow Springs Lake, 158 acres, 7520 ft.
    Black Canyon Lake, 78 acres, 7560 ft.

Tonto Creek System
    None

Sierra Anchas
    None

Canyon, Cibecue, Carrizo Creeks
    Blue Lake, 3 acres, 7300 ft.
    Wildhorse Lake, 2acres 7300 ft.
    Cooley Tank, 5 acres, 7050 ft.
    Bootleg Lake, 5 acres, 6800 ft.

White River System
    Big Bear (Shush Be Tou) Lake, 18 acres, 7800 ft.
    Little Bear (Shush Be Zahze) Lake, 15 acres, 7900 ft.
    Hawley Lake, 260 acres, 8200 f.t
    Cyclone Lake, 37 acres, 8150 ft.
    Christmas Tree Lake 40, acres, 8200 feet
    Earl Park Lake, 38 acres, 8250 ft.
    A-1 Lake, 24 acres, 8800 ft.
    Horseshoe Cienega Lake, 120 acres, 8200 ft.

Bog Tank, 18 acres, 8200 ft.
Sunrise Lake, 875 acres, 9130 ft.

Bonito Creek Drainage
    Corn Creek Tank, 8 acres, 6300 ft.
    Tonto Lake, 82 acres, 7000 ft.
    Hurricane Lake, 19 acres, 8940 ft.

Black River Drainage
    Big Lake. 450 acres, 9000 ft.
    Crescent Lake, 100 acres, 9040 ft.
    Basin Lake, 30 acres, 9000 ft.
    Sierra Blanca Lake, 5 acres, 8400 ft
    Ackre Lake, 2 acres, 8850 ft.
    Reservation Lake, 280 acres, 9040 ft.
    Drift Fence Lake, 16 acres, 8900 ft.
    Pacheta Lake, 65 acres, 8200 ft.
    Seneca Lake, 25 acres, 5000 ft. (drains into Salt River)

Little Colorado River System
    Bunch Reservoir, 20 acres, 8260 ft.
    River Reservoir, 50 acres, 8220 ft.
    Tunnel Reservoir, 15 acres, 8260 ft.
    White Mountain Reservoir, 20 acres to 450 acres, 9200 ft.
    Carnero Reservoir, 65 acres when full, 9000 ft.
    Mexican Hay Lake, 100 acres when full, 8900 ft.
    Becker Lake, 85 acres, 6900 ft.
    Lee Valley Lake, 35 acres, 9420 ft.
    Coulter Reservoir, 5 acres max. , 9200 ft.
    Concho Reservoir, 60 acres, 6300 ft.
    White Mountain Lake (private water), 80 acres, 5950 ft.
    Nelson Reservoir, 60 acres, 7410 ft.
    Hulsey Lake, 3 acres, 8620 ft.
    Rainbow Lake, 65 acres, 6700 ft.
    Woodland Lake, 18 acres, 6900 ft.
    Show Low Lake, 100 acres, 6540 ft.
    Scott Reservoir, 80 acres, 6700 ft.
    Fools Hollow Lake, 150 acres, 6300 ft.
    Ashurst Lake, 200 acres, 7100 ft.
    Kinnikinick Lake, 120 acres, 7040 ft.

San Francisco River System
    Luna Lake, 75 acres, 7890 ft.

Eagle Creek Drainage
    Point of Pines Lake, 27 acres, 6200 feet
    Pine Flat Tank, 3 acres, 6000 ft.
    Maggie Jones Tank, 2 acres, 5600 ft.

Blue River System
    None

Mt. Graham
    Snow Flat Lake, 1 acre, 8900 ft.
    Riggs Flat Lake, 11 acres, 9000 ft.
    Frye Mesa Reservoir, 4 acres, 4840 ft.
    Cluff Ranch Pond Number Three, 10 acres, 3320 ft.
    Roper Lake, 32 acres, 3140 ft.

Chiricahua Mountains
    Rucker Lake, filled, 6000 ft. (no fish)

Santa Catalina Mountains
    Rose Canyon Lake, 7 acres, 7000 ft.

Chuska Mountains
    Tsaile Lake, 260 acres, 7050 ft.
    Wheatfields Lake, 270 acres, 7300 ft.
    Round Rock Lake, 50 acres, 5600 ft.
    Antelope Lake, 3 acres, 5300 ft.
    Chuska Lake, 25 acres, 6900 ft.
    Blue Canyon Lake, 60 acres, 8800 ft.
    Assayi Lake, 56 acres, 8900 ft.
    Aspen Pond, 1acre, 7000 ft.
    Berland Lake, 3 acres, 8800 ft.
    Trout Lake, 26 acres, 8900 ft.
    Long Lake, 50 acres, 8950 ft.
    Toadachene Lake, 20 acres, 8700 ft.
    Little White Cove Lake, 40 acres, 7700 ft.

Bill Williams River Drainage
    Dogtown Reservoir, 3 acres, 7070 ft.
    Cataract Lake, 35 acres, 6800 ft.
    Kaibab Lake, 45 acres, 6790 ft.
    Santa Fe Lake, 3 acres, 6940 ft.
    Perkins Tank, 2 acres, 6820 ft.

Sonoita-Santa Cruz Drainages
    Peña Blanca Lake, 50 acres, 3900 ft.
    Parker Canyon Lake, 90 acres, 5200 feet
    Sonoita Lake, 150 acres, 3800 ft.